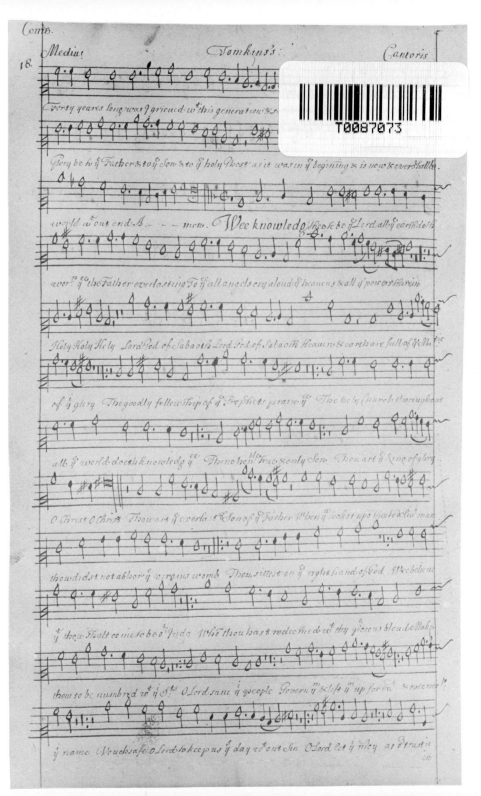

A Study

of the

BING-GOSTLING PART BOOKS

in the

Library of York Minster

together with

a Systematic Catalogue

by

Watkins Shaw
Honorary Librarian
St Michael's College, Tenbury
1948-85

Published for the
Oxford University Press
Walton Street Oxford OX2 6D[

C O N T E N T S

LIST OF PLATES

Frontispiece and between pp. 22 & 23

INTRODUCTION

The Library of the Dean and Chapter of York Minster stands possessed of eight volumes of manuscript forming a set, uniform in size (30.5 x 19.5 cms more or less) containing a repertory of English cathedral music of the period c1570-1695. Respectively (though with some irregularity) the volumes furnish the separate voice parts for Medius, Contratenor, Tenor, and Bassus, each for both sides of a choir, decani and cantoris. While they have all been subject to repair and cropping, each book substantially retains its late 17th-century leather binding. The present collective library reference is M.l.S.

They have for some considerable time been known as the 'Gostling' part-books because they formed part of the collection of William Gostling (c1695-1777), Minor Canon of Canterbury Cathedral, whose signature and book-plate is found in each.[1] As will presently appear, however, there is an earlier and closer Gostling connection. William Gostling's significant collection ('musicae reconditae eximiaeque locuples') was sold by Langford, as traced by A. Hyatt King, Some British Collectors of Music (Cambridge, 1963), on 26 and 27 May 1777 (not by Flackton, as stated in the Dictionary of National Biography), and in the unique surviving copy of the sale catalogue, now Hirsch IV, 1083 in the Music Room of the British Library (Reference Division), the following description of Lot 82 undoubtedly refers to these volumes:

> A complete Choir set of Anthems and Services, by the more
> early Composers for the Church, in 8 vol. written by Sub-
> Dean Gostling.

The reference to 'Sub-Dean Gostling' will be elucidated below.

It is not known who acquired them in 1777 nor how the books reached York. They were listed in the York Minster Catalogue of 1850 with the remark 'These are part Books for a Choir and most beautifully written'.[2] The first scholars of any importance to consult them were the editors of _Tudor Church Music_ (1922-29) who, however, in saying they were 'Begun about the middle of the seventeenth century' dated them earlier than can be justified.

By whom, when, and for what purpose were these books compiled, and what is their significance?

To answer the first question we must rely on the testimony of handwriting, of which three types are exhibited, shown respectively in Plates I, II, and V. Inside the front cover of the Bassus Cantoris book is a brief memorandum (Plate III) relating to 28 April 1679 made by one 'Steph. Bing', and this clearly identifies him as the scribe of hand II (Plate II). Readers of biographies of Purcell [3] will recognise the name Stephen Bing as that of one who copied music for Westminster Abbey in the 1670's, and enquiry reveals the following entry in the Abbey unofficial register under the date 26 November 1681:

> Mr Steven Bing dyed and buried the 1st day of December at Canterbury.[4]

Pursuing this, the burial of 'Mr. Stephen Bing' on that date may be traced at St George's Church, Canterbury. In his Will[5] dated 12 February 1680/81 he asked to be buried there near his father and mother, a fairly certain hint that he may have been baptised in that parish; and so it proves. 'Stephan, son of Stephan Binge' was baptised at St George's on 20 September 1610.[6] His Will describes him as 'Clerk one of the Minor Canons of St Paul's London', and in sum these clues enable us to piece his career together as follows.

He was a chorister of Canterbury Cathedral, first named
as such in the accounting year ending Michaelmas 1618 and
last mentioned in the year ending 1624 when his name, though
entered in the fair copy accounts, was struck through. It
seems that he did not proceed to sing as a man in Canterbury
Cathedral choir in any of the various capacities of melody
man, substitute, lay clerk, or minor canon,[7] and we lose
trace of him for some 17 years. But he evidently acquired
Holy Orders, and in the year ending Midsummer 1642 his
name occurs for the first time at St Paul's Cathedral
when, in the Accounts of the College of Minor Canons,[8] he
signed for his dividend that year. He was still there
when the last dividend before the Interregnum was distri-
buted at Midsummer 1649.

A glimpse of his interests is provided by a contemporary
pencil memorandum in these accounts for 1646-47: 'Lent
Mr Binge ye 23º of July 1647 Morlyes Introduction' (i.e.,
A Plaine and Easie Introduction to Practicall Musicke
by Thomas Morley, 1597). But his tenure at St Paul's was
interrupted by the cessation of Prayer Book worship and
the abolition of capitular bodies. Apparently he stayed
in London, and he figures in John Playford's list, given
in A Musicall Banquet, 1651, of 'excellent and able Masters'
then available to give tuition, he being named 'For Voyce
and Viole'. His association with viol music is supported
by his MS transcription of 3-part 'Fantazies & Aires' by
Jenkins, Locke, and Young[9] of which more will presently
be said (see p.8). Meanwhile, the Trustees for the Main-
tenance of Ministers (a Commonwealth body) allotted him
pittances of £4 and £2 in 1655 and 1657 respectively.[10]

He was on the spot immediately St Paul's Cathedral began
to function again upon the Restoration in 1660 when he
and a certain Henry Smith were the only two surviving
Minor Canons in priest's orders (the third survivor,

Randolph Jewett, was only a deacon). It was arranged that
he should exchange his existing patent as a simple Minor
Canon for a new one as Minor Canon and Senior Cardinal,
and he was admitted as such on 14 May 1661.[11] For the first
two years after the Restoration he was also Warden of the
College of Minor Canons, and the accounts of that body for
the years ending Midsummer 1661 and 1662 are carefully
written by him.

Once more, however, his work was to be interrupted, this
time by the destruction of St Paul's Cathedral in the Fire
of London, 1666. Though the choir ceased to function prop-
erly for some 30 years, the Minor Canons, being in occupa-
tion of a freehold, still qualified for their annual
dividend, and their accounts show that Bing collected this
in 1671 to 1681 inclusive (years ending at Midsummer) and
he was allowed it posthumously for 1682. But the men of
the choir were permitted to seek employment elsewhere for
the time being, and on 21 March 1666/7 Bing was appointed
a Senior Vicar Choral (i.e., a vicar in Holy Orders) at
Lincoln Cathedral.[12] There, so far as is known, he remained until an opportunity occurred to return to London and
he was admitted as a Lay Vicar of Westminster Abbey on
1 April 1672 when he signed the Precentor's Book.[13] The
Abbey accounts[14] give us glimpses of his activity in copying music there, surviving vestiges of which are referred
to in Appendix I infra.

Year ending Michaelmas

1673	To Stephen Bing for ruled papyr for a set of Quirebooks . . . £2
1676	To Mr Bing for Books for the Church for ye last year 1675 then omitted . . . xxxiil ls vid
1679	To Mr Bing for writing 29 sheets and 23 staves . . . xxxviijs

He remained in his dual capacity of Minor Canon of St
Paul's and Lay Vicar of Westminster Abbey until his death
in November 1681.[15]

   Thus far we have followed the clue of Plate III and its
identification of the scribe of Plate II. What of the hand
shown in Plate I, that of the earliest entries in the book?
This, too, despite its differences, is that of Bing, as
revealed by comparison with the Accounts of the College of
Minor Canons of St Paul's Cathedral which Stephen Bing
wrote out for 1661 and 1662 (see Plate IV; any remote possibility that there were two men of that name at St Paul's
either concurrently or successively is quite ruled out on
the evidence of the muniments).

   The overall impression on comparing the two styles of
hand is of greater cursiveness in Plates I and IV as
against more angular stiffness in Plates II and III. More
detailed comparison shows that in general the minuscules
g, w, and y, for example, are distinguished thus: in the
hand of Plates I and IV the 'g' is more likely to have a
sloping, simply looped descender, the 'w' more likely to
be rounded in formation, the 'y' almost always formed like
a 'u' together with a simple downward stroke for descender,
while the ascender of a 'd' may be either vertical or
backward looping. By contrast, the hand of Plates II and III
tends to have a 'g' with a tightly curled descender, a 'w'
formed more like a double 'v', and a 'y' with a sharp
angle between two separate strokes, of which the descender
slopes markedly backward and under, while the ascender of
a 'd' is almost without exception stiffly upright.

   But it will also be observed that even within one and
the same document the descender of the 'g' can vary,
notably in Bing's own name, so that the hand of Plate IV
reveals this now with a 'g' as in that of Plates II and

III, now as in that of Plate I. Yet, examining his signatures in various years in the St Paul's accounts we find
sometimes one, sometimes the other (in the Precentor's
Book of Westminster Abbey we find the 'g' with the sloping,
simply looped descender, the only signature of his to survive at the Abbey). And although many pages of the York
books are differentiated from each other in the two styles
of Plates I and II respectively, others show signs of
instability in this respect. Thus, in the Tenor Cantoris
book, Farrant's 'High' Service, in the style of Plate I,
shows besides the 'g' characteristic of that style, a
form of this minuscule associated with Plates II and III;
while in Rogers's Service in G the Creed has 'y' in the
style of Plate I, but Magnificat shows that of Plate II.
Furthermore, though the Viol Fantasies which, as already
mentioned, Bing transcribed have only a minimum of verbal
text, they too exhibit sometimes the more flowing cursive
of Plate I, and sometimes the stiffer manner of Plate II,
e.g. (Treble book, f.1) 'Mr Joh: Jenkins's Fansies of 3
Parts' compared with (Bass book, f.19) 'Mr Math: Locks
Fansies & Aires of 3 Parts'.

All in all, therefore, despite a first general impression of separate scribes, it must be concluded that Plates
I and II simply represent different styles of one and the
same hand, and that everything in the York books except
items in the hand of Plate V was written by Stephen Bing.

The hand of Plate V is easily identified as that of
John Gostling, and can be authenticated by reference to
his signatures in the Accounts of the College of Minor
Canons of St Paul's Cathedral, his endorsement on the
fly-leaf of Egerton MS 2959 in the Reference Division of
the British Library, and, most freely, in the Parish
Register, now in Canterbury Cathedral Library, which he
maintained as Vicar of Littlebourne. John Gostling is a

better-known figure than Bing, and so his career can be more succinctly described.

He is likely to be the John Gostling who was admitted to St John's College, Cambridge in October 1668. Having been ordained at what would seem to be almost the earliest canonical age, he was admitted Minor Canon of Canterbury Cathedral in November 1675, probably after a year's probation, and appointed Vicar of Littlebourne, Kent at the same time. Described as 'a base from Canterbury, Master of Arts', he was sworn a Gentleman of the Chapel Royal on 28 February 1678/9, and on 23 January 1681/2 (hard on Bing's death) he began a probationary year as a Minor Canon of St Paul's Cathedral, being later admitted Sub-dean there on 15 January 1689/90 - which last appointment explains the expression recorded above from the W. Gostling Sale Catalogue of 1777.[16] He retained these various posts as well as his living at Littlebourne until his death at an advanced age in 1733.

It is the fact of John Gostling's handwriting in the York books which gives them a stronger Gostling connection than that simply of their possession by William Gostling. They must have passed into John Gostling's hands on Bing's death, doubtless because of the St Paul's Cathedral link between the two men, and they naturally passed to his son William on his own death.

The elder Gostling is known as a transcriber of music apart from the York books. A large album in score, now in the Humanities Research Center of the University of Texas, Austin, USA, is a personal collection of anthems based on the Chapel Royal repertory of 1670-1705.[17] A small MS in the Euing Collection, University of Glasgow (R.d.47) consists of secular songs for bass, of interest to him as a renowned basso profundo for whom Purcell's

'They that go down to the sea in ships' was conceived.
A book of organ parts to anthems which he copied c1705-10
is MU.MS 669 in the Fitzwilliam Museum, Cambridge, and
a stray bass voice part of Blow's 'I beheld, and lo! a
great multitude' is now Tenbury MS 1225. There are also
three pages (50-52) in his writing (Blow, 'Sing we merrily';
Wise, 'O praise God in his holiness') in a bass part-book,
E10-20, at Canterbury Cathedral, and a good deal of his
work can be seen in surviving part-books at St Paul's
Cathedral (see Appendix II infra). But his largest legacy
of church music in part-books is found in Tenbury MSS
797-803 and 1176-82 deposited in the Bodleian Library,
Oxford, about which something will be said presently.

If, as his own memorandum indicates, Bing was working
on these books in April 1679, then he may well have done
so almost up to his death in November 1681, which gives
the latest date for the transcripts in his hand. When did
he begin the books? The distinction between 'Mr Rogers'
and 'Dr Rogers' within the space of some 15 leaves early
on in each book may suggest that he started not long before
Rogers acquired his doctorate in July 1669 (unless, trans-
cribing later than that, he mechanically copied 'Mr Rogers'
from the document in front of him). That he was not writing
much before 1670 is indicated by his description of Thomas
Tudway as organist of King's College, Cambridge in the
section devoted to verse anthems, an appointment Tudway
took up in the autumn of 1670. The same impression is given
by a sectional heading in the earlier Plate I hand of
Bing, 'A Collection of...Anthems...made at Lincoln...
(16)68, 69, & 70' (Medius Decani, f.83). As Bing was at
Westminster Abbey from 1672 reliance may be placed on
his distinction between 'Mr Blow' and 'Dr Blow', and this
shows that nearly all of the works by Blow in his hand
were transcribed before December 1677. These consider-
ations lead one to conclude that he began the books about

1668-70 while at Lincoln, brought them with him on his return to London, and copied the most considerable substance in them between 1672 and 1678, but may have continued his transcriptions until shortly before his death.

Gostling's additions are obviously later than 1681, and he was still using the books after William Turner took his doctorate in 1696 and late enough to copy Blow's 'My God, my God', composed 6 September 1697. But because 'Dr Turner' and this anthem by Blow come at almost the latest point of Gostling's entries, and he gives nothing by Clarke or Croft, he probably abandoned these books somewhat before 1700.

As to the function of the books, it is obvious that they were not designed for, and are incapable of use in, practical performance from choir stalls. Even when they are most carefully written, the stave ruling and the space between the staves is too close for that purpose. Choir books of this period have more generous staves permitting larger note heads, and more space between staves making for ease in reading the words. When, on a preliminary leaf of the Tenor Decani book, Bing wrote 'A Book of Services and Anthems for a Quire' he was referring to contents, not format. Furthermore, in a true set of choir books even a four-part composition would be copied twice to provide for both 'decani' and 'cantoris'. In the York books Bing begins conscientiously by doing this, but presently realises it is unnecessary for his purpose so long as each of the four parts is represented once, as in Blow's 'O how amiable'. In a five-part work (say MAATB), for choir book purposes M, T, and B would each be entered in both sets of books together with A(I) in the Decani book and A(II) in the Cantoris book, but it is enough for Bing that he writes William Mundy's five-part Service in all four Decani books and uses the Cantoris books only for

the additional alto part. Byrd's six-part 'Sing joyfully'
is correspondingly treated, and there are other examples.
When copying Gibbons's 'Hosanna to the Son of David' Bing
went so far as to write the unison Tenor part in both books,
but then, realising the position at that point, did not
trouble to duplicate the unison Bass part. A further con-
sideration against use in choir stalls is that at times
his script becomes very cramped, and his text contains
various annotations and some supplementary slips of inserted paper, making reading difficult. As for Gostling's
contributions, his script is frankly informal, and by the
time the books reached him they were becoming so full that
in some instances (e.g., Purcell's 'O God, thou art my God',
a five-part work) he could only find room for the two Tenor
parts by putting them both into the Cantoris book. Finally,
for practical use they would have required much better
indexing.

The fact is that these books are the file copies of a
professional transcriber, from which on request he could
draw the large fair copies needed for a choir in performance. It happens that this state of affairs is precisely
confirmed by Tenbury MSS 797-803 and 1176-82, both written
by Gostling. The former set consists of seven books out
of an original eight, as at York, and they exhibit the
same sort of narrow stave ruling and minimum space between
the staves; the latter set is generous in both respects
with carefully formed notes and clear words. And the significant point is that the repertory in the larger set
(1176-82) is very substantially drawn from the contents
of the smaller set (797-803) thus demonstrating the existence of a file set belonging to the copyist and a choir
set drawn therefrom, presumably as a commission. That both
sets are now in the same library is probably fortuitous.[18]

The contents transcribed by Bing may be considered from
more than one point of view. But first there is the minor
point that they testify to free-lance copying of parts for
cathedral (etc.) choirs. One would have supposed that, in
the normal way, a copyist would, as a set task, draw out
parts for a given choir (as Bing himself did for Westminster
Abbey and St Paul's Cathedral) from specified compositions
supplied to him for the purpose, and it is by no means
easy to see what market there could have been for the work
of the owners of such file copies as these. But here
appears to be evidence that such a possibility was envis-
aged. Copies for personal use would surely have been in
score. What we do not know is whether, when copying for
the Abbey or St Paul's, Bing transcribed from these books,
or whether he assembled them as a result of doing that
work.

However that may be, as the period of their compilation
can be defined, broadly speaking, within c1670-c1680, it
might be hoped that they would help towards the dating of
works by composers then active, Blow, Purcell, Turner,
and Wise. And so they might, if no other evidence were
forthcoming. But a list of music copied into the books
of the Chapel Royal between 1670 and 1676[19] firmly provides
narrower limits than Bing's transcripts, and the amount
of other music transcribed elsewhere by William Tucker
(see Appendix I _infra_) necessarily testifies to its having
been composed before his death in 1679. For John Blow
these books tell us that 'God be merciful' and 'I will
cry unto thee' probably pre-date December 1677; they are
the prime testimony to a date earlier than December 1681
for Purcell's 'Give sentence with me', 'O praise the Lord,
all ye heathen', and 'Save me, O God', as also for Wise's
Services in D minor and E major and his 'Blessed is the
man'. It is possible that they may help a little also with
some works by William Turner.

Next, Bing's choice of works for his collection suggests
some points of interest in relation both to those composed
before the Civil War and Commonwealth, and to those written
after the Restoration of Charles II in 1660.

So far as the earlier group is concerned he evidently
assumed that his potential clients would not have access
to Barnard's First Book of Selected Church Musick (1641),
even though, as we know, a stock of that publication survived the Interregnum; for among a considerable number of
Barnard's items Bing included all the Full Anthems except
Byrd's 'O God, whom our offences', Sheppard's 'Haste thee,
O God', and Tallis's 'Wipe away my sins'. But it may be
significant of the taste for which he was catering that he
chose only three of the ten Verse Anthems published by
Barnard. As to Services, of Barnard's 15 Bing covers six,
none of them a verse Service.

Yet, on the other hand, Bing gives Services from this
period not published by Barnard, as follows: Amner (2),
Batten, J.Farrant, R.Farrant, Patrick, Portman, and T.
Tomkins. Further, he copied anthems not found in Barnard's
publication thus: Batten (13), Bull (2), Byrd (1), Dering (1),
O.Gibbons (6), W.Lawes (2), Morley (1), Portman (2), Ramsey (2),
J.Tomkins (1), T.Tomkins (5), Ward (3), R. or W.White (1).
In addition, there are some less well-known figures like
Ed(ward) Smith and Thomas Wilkinson.

Traces of the repertory of pre-Civil War music in use
at Westminster Abbey after the Restoration survive in frag-
ments (significantly, in Bing's hand) of a contemporary
choir book, Tenor Decani '5', discussed in Appendix I infra.
Here we find four Services and 18 Anthems composed before
c1640, all save one Service and one Anthem being in the
York books also. Bearing in mind that the testimony of this
single Westminster Abbey book is fragmentary only, it may

well be that the correspondence between the books now at York and the Abbey repertory of this class of music in the 1670's was in fact greater. If so, then to the extent that we now lack evidence of the nature of that repertory it may well be supplied by the York books.

If it is clear that there is some correspondence between Bing's books and the Abbey repertory in this regard, want of comprehensive evidence makes its impossible to say whether, or to what extent, it may have been shared by the Chapel Royal in the 1670's. But, moving to music of the later period, taking in that of senior men such as Child, C.Gibbons, Locke, Rogers, and Tucker as well as the rising young men of that decade - Aldrich, Blow, Humfrey, Turner, Wise, and the still youthful Henry Purcell - we find that the central and substantial core of Bing's repertory is closely related to that of both Westminster Abbey and the Chapel Royal at this time, ignoring, not unexpectedly, the special category of 'anthems with symphonies' that was distinctive of the Chapel Royal alone. Testimony to this is directly to hand, firstly in two part-books (Alto Cantoris 'No 1A' and Tenor Cantoris 'No 4') surviving at Westminster Abbey which contains items copied between c1670 and the death of William Tucker in 1679 (see Appendix I infra). Secondly, this is supported by the list of music copied into the books of the Chapel Royal 1670-76 (see footnote 19). Bing gives all the Services named there and among the Anthems he includes all those by Blow, C.Gibbons, Humfrey,[20] Tucker, and Turner, and nearly all of those by Child and Wise, a substantial total of 49 anthems in common.

Beyond that central correspondence, however, Bing's York part-books display some individual characteristics. His representation of Christopher Gibbons and Turner is somewhat stronger than at the Chapel and Abbey so far as

present knowledge goes, and he takes cognisance of some
lesser composers like Henry Hall and William King as well
as of the odd figure of Silas Taylor. He also seems exceptional in choosing as many as six works by George Jeffreys.
His inclusion of fairly numerous anthems by Hecht and Cutts
is not only a reminder of his own connection with Lincoln
Cathedral, of which Hecht became organist in c1663 and
Cutts a Junior Vicar Choral in 1664, but of the existence
of provincial composers unrecognised in the metropolis,
so helping us to see the period in better perspective.[21]

Finally there is the matter of the textual value of
Bing's transcripts. The lack of an organ part is obviously
a serious gap in the complete text of a verse anthem.[22]
Otherwise two elements are in play here, the nature of the
sources available to a scribe and the extent of his reliability as a faithful copyist.

About the first of these it is impossible to generalise,
as it will vary with different parts of Bing's repertory.
Separate judgments concerning individual works or groups
of works must be made by specialist textual scholars in
relation to whatever other sources of ascertainable authority are available. A few superficial points suggest
themselves, however. Where pre-Civil War music is involved
there may well be a prima facie case to consider whether
a scribe working c1670 may not have been relying on Barnard's
1641 publication. Only careful sifting could settle that,
so possibly separating scribal slips from readings of independent authority. But it may be significant that in
copying at least one group of works included by Barnard
in 1641 Bing preserves exactly the same sequence of works.

Barnard's publication, however, includes by no means all
the pre-Civil War music in these part-books, and it is an
open question whence Bing derived his text of the remainder.

In the 20th century editors have been able to draw, _inter_
alia, on pre-Civil War MSS at Peterhouse, Cambridge and
on MSS of similar date and of early post-Restoration date
at Durham Cathedral, none of them available to Bing. Even
if - a pure guess - he had access to Barnard's manuscript
books (RCM MSS 1045-51) these would by no means have
supplied all he needed. Whatever the reliability or prov-
enance of his transcripts, it would seem that they represent a line of transmission independent of other early
post-Restoration sources of these works.

In the particular instance of Thomas Tomkins, Bing
plainly implies that he had access to a source other than
Musica Deo Sacra (1668), and that must be the publication
he means when he annotates his transcripts by reference
to what he calls 'ye printed books'. How far Nathaniel
Tomkins's publication of his father's work in 1668 is
regarded as being of the purest essence, I do not know;
but it is certainly interesting, and perhaps significant,
to find traces of its circulation independent of that
publication.

Reaching music closely contemporary with the date of
his copying, one cannot but suppose that Bing obtained
text of Blow, Humfrey, Turner, Wise, and, later, Purcell
from sources close to the composer; and it is evident that
he took some opportunity, at least, to compare his work
with other authoritative transcripts. The fact remains,
of course, that where (as with Blow, for instance) we have
manuscripts in the composer's own hand, such copies as
these of Bing are of far less significance (I do not say
no significance at all). But otherwise, at face value, for
this school of composers they are of no less significance
so far as they go than those in, for example, MU.MS 117
in the Fitzwilliam Museum, which also represent one remove
from a prime source. And it is by the single thread of

Bing's testimony that one work, 'Give sentence with me', by Henry Purcell hangs.

On the question of his reliability in copying, he was sufficiently interested in what he was doing to make textual annotations here and there, and the neatness of his earlier entries makes a very good impression. But there are uncomfortable signs of lack of order, and there is a disturbing number of incomplete texts. Even his heading about anthems composed at Lincoln, 1668-70 in the Medius Decani book is not repeated in the other books. In general, while his transcripts certainly merit attention and must be taken into account when no over-riding other authority is available, it may be suggested that perhaps he should be regarded circumspectly, with the possibility of error, not only alternative readings worth collation, in mind.

ACKNOWLEDGMENTS

I am most grateful to the Librarian and other officers of York Minster Library for agreeable and friendly facilities when consulting the manuscripts in their care, and for permission to reproduce Plate I, II, III, and V. I similarly acknowledge the kindness of the Librarians of Westminster Abbey and St Paul's Cathedral, and the permission of the Custos of the College of Minor Canons of St Paul's to reproduce Plate IV.

REFERENCES

1. His book-plate embodies a coat-of-arms, 'Gules, a chevron ermine
    between 3 crescents argent', executed in trick. This seems to
    have been made up and assumed by approximation to two slightly
    different achievements of arms associated with the names
    Gos(s)elyn, Gosling, Gooseling and Gosselin.

2. Information kindly supplied by Mr David Griffiths.

3. W.H.Cummings, Purcell (1881); J.A.Westrup, Purcell (1937 and
    subsequent revisions).

4. J.L.Chester, The Marriage, Baptismal, and Burial Registers of
    the ... Abbey of St Peter, Westminster (1876).

5. Public Record Office PROB 11/368/179 (olim 179 North).

6. See The Registers of St George the Martyr, Canterbury, ed.
    J.M.Cowper (Canterbury 1891). One 'Steven Bing' whom we take
    to be the father, was buried there on 31 August 1632, and
    'Mary Binge', a widow and probably the mother was buried on
    3 February 1637/8. Other entries appear to show that our
    subject was the only son and second child of five.

7. Canterbury Cathedral, Fair copy accounts Nos 26-47, 1617-42
    (with gaps); Bound papers of accounts, 1576-1642 (with gaps).

8. Guildhall Library, London, St Paul's Cathedral Muniments, F.B.6.

9. Guildhall Library, London, Gresham College Collection, G Mus 469-71.

10. A.G.Matthews, Walker Revised, 1948.

11. Guildhall Library, London, St Paul's Cathedral Muniments,
    Minute Book 1660-64, F.C.1; Muniment Book 1660-95, W.C.45.

12. Guildhall Library, London, St Paul's Cathedral Muniments,
    Minute Book F.C.2, 22 November 1666; Lincolnshire County
    Record Office, Lincoln Cathedral Chapter Acts A.3.11, f. 254.

13. W(estminster) A(bbey) M(uniments) 61228A, f. 130

14. W.A.M. 33706, 33710, 33714.

15. Sir Jack Westrup strenuously opposed the idea that Bing
    combined these two capacities and considered that there were
    two men of the same name. The matter is discussed in an
    End-note on p.21 .

16. For all these details, see J. & J.A.Venn, Alumni Cantabrigienses,
    Part 1, (Cambridge, 1922); The Old Cheque Book of the Chapel
    Royal, ed. E.F.Rimbault, (1872); Guildhall Library, London,
    St Paul's Cathedral Muniment Book 1660-95 (W.C.45), ff. 175, 219v.
    With regard to the post of Sub-dean it should be said, lest
    this be misunderstood, that it does not mean he was an important
    functionary as deputy to the Dean. Among the minor canons there
    were offices which, as it were, mirrored in parvo those of the

dignitaries - for the Precentor there was the Succentor; for the Treasurer there was the Sacrist; and to complete the pattern though (unlike the others) without corresponding duties, for the Dean there was the Sub-dean.

17. For a discussion of this document, see my review in Music & Letters, vol. 61 (1980), pp. 487-90, of the published facsimile.

18. The repertory in 797-803, the 'file set', suggests that Gostling moved over from the York set to this c1700. The much earlier and famous set of part-books compiled by John Barnard before the Civil War (now in the Royal College of Music,(MSS 1045-51) also constitute a transcriber's file, not choir books, in just the same way, though they were also used as printer's copy for The First Book of Selected Church Musick (1641). Barnard, the compiler of these books c1622-38, was a Minor Canon of St Paul's Cathedral, and from 1642 Bing was one of his junior colleagues. Barnard does not appear to have survived the Interregnum. Is it fanciful to wonder whether RCM MSS 1045-51 passed from Barnard to Bing as a result of this association, and then, along with Bing's other books now at York, to John Gostling by a like association, with the result that both sets now carry the bookplate of William Gostling?

19. H.C.de Lafontaine, The King's Musick (London, 1909), pp. 305-7.

20. At the mention of Humfrey's name the reader may have hesitated after the recent references to anthems with symphonies. Though Humfrey's works were indeed performed in the Chapel Royal with symphonies, the fact is that the York part-books taken together with those at Westminster Abbey make it clear that even at this early date they were used elsewhere without them. Some loss is involved in their omission, but these symphonies are completely detachable without causing the structure to collapse, except, to some degree in 'By the waters of Babylon', and here, in spite of the strictures that have been passed upon it, the adaptation for organ only as given in a copy in the hand of no less a person than Purcell (British Library (Reference Division), Add. MS 30932, f.52) must have been that employed for this anthem outside the Chapel Royal in conjunction with voice parts such as Bing transmits.

21. Thus also Tenbury MS 1442 (deposited in the Bodleian Library), of similar date, which includes among a general repertory works by Silver, Holmes, and Jewett, composers of local repute in Winchester and Salisbury.

22. Bing's part-books are not alone in this. Neither the printed nor the manuscript sets of Barnard have any associated organ book, and indeed there are indications generally that the compilation of organ parts was a job left to the organists, independent of the copying sets of voice parts. The organ books forming part of Tenbury MSS 1176-82 seem to be exceptional in this respect.

End-note.   Bing as Lay Vicar of Westminster Abbey

Two objections might be raised to the identification of Stephen
(Steven) Bing, Lay Vicar of Westminster Abbey, with Stephen Bing,
Minor Canon of St Paul's Cathedral.

   First, it might be said that a minor canon, being a clergyman,
would not hold a post as a lay singingman. There is no substance
in this. No legal barrier exists, and at that time the distinction
between a minor canon (or vicar-choral in Holy Orders) and a lay
singingman was far less than now, all minor canons taking their
full part as choir singers and not confining themselves to intoning
the priest's part of the services. There is, moreover, a known parallel.
Randolph Jewett, likewise Minor Canon of St Paul's at the time of
the Great Fire, availed himself of permission to take up work elsewhere and went to Winchester Cathedral to take up the post of
organist, for which Holy Orders were not required. There he stayed
until his death, and, like Bing, he continued to qualify for his
dividend as Minor Canon of St Paul's. A lay vicar received less
stipend than a minor canon, it is true; but Bing, still secure in
his St Paul's dividend, was well placed to ignore that for the sake
of an opportunity to get back to London from Lincoln.

   Second, there is the curious fact that the Accounts of Westminster
Abbey show Bing as a lay vicar for the years ending Michaelmas 1682
and 1683, that is to say after his death. Inspection of these Accounts
in general easily disposes of this difficulty.

   They listed the officers in order of seniority. In the year following the death of, say, the third in seniority his name would be
omitted, all the others would move up by one line, and a new name
added at the bottom of the list. But it was sufficient for the clerk
to account for the right number of stipends, and he was not in-
variably watchful about names. A case in point crystallises this.
William Tucker, Minor Canon of Westminster, died in February 1678/9,
but in the Accounts ending at Michaelmas 1679 the clerk left his

name undisturbed. Then, at Michaelmas 1680 and 1681 his name, which
had been third in seniority out of four, is omitted, and that of
Thomas Linacre comes in as fourth in seniority. So far, so good: but
at Michaelmas 1682 Tucker's name reappears in its old position and
Linacre is not mentioned.

In view of the entry of the death of a 'Steven Bing' in the unofficial Register of the Abbey, the identity of the signature in the
Precentor's Book there with specimens at St Paul's Cathedral, one has
no difficulty in supposing that the clerk of the 1682 and 1683
Accounts was not watchful enough to omit Bing's name when copying
his list (maybe with last year's in front of him) and to bring in
that of his successor.

W: Gostling.

Munday ye 28 Ap: 79. about 1 of ye clock in ye day time wee Mr Wardens well
was opened in ye & price of ye Principle of Cliffords Inn & one Steph: Bing

The Accompt of Stephen Bund'are Burd'are Warden of ye
Colledge of ye 12 Other Canons of St Pauls Church London of all ye
Receipts & rents he hath rec'd unto him & or belonging to ye Colledge
As allso the Expenses he hath expended for & upon ye Colledge aforesaid
from ye Feast of St John the Baptist 1660 (at or about ye time it
pleased Almighty God by ye Gracious King Charles the 2d to restore
ye Church to its rights & reverences) unto ye same Feast of St John 1661.

expended more than rec'd

Stephen Bing
Henry Smyth

19.
22.

IV

CATALOGUE

Explanatory notes

In the lists which follow, names of composers are given
exactly as found in the manuscripts, except that Christian
names have been added here and there to avoid confusion,
and abbreviated Christian names have been expanded. Both
these types of addition are in italic. But a few Christian names - 'Ben', 'Thos', 'Will/Wm/Willm' - have been
left so, as not having the oddity of some others. Where
no name is attached to any item in the manuscripts, this
has been supplied in one of two ways: (a) in brackets,
from the Index to the book in question; (b) in italic,
from some other source of identification.

The titles of Services are also given exactly as found,
but with occasional clarification (in italic), as for
example 'in E minor'.

The first words of Anthems have been modernised, chiefly
in accordance with the Book of Common Prayer.

In the Index, modern standardised forms of names ('Byrd'
- reluctantly - for 'Bird') and designations of Services
are used.

The components of Services are indicated by numerals,
thus:

(1)	Venite, exultemus Domino
(2)	Te Deum, laudamus
(3)	Bendicite, omnia opera
(4)	Benedictus Dominus
(5)	Jubilate Deo
(6)	Responses to Commandments
(7)	Creed
(8)	Magnificat
(9)	Cantate Domino
(10)	Nunc Dimittis
(11)	Deus Misereatur

The sign * distinguishes items in the hand of John
Gostling.

(1) Medius Decani

Inside front cover: Signature 'W.Gostling' and bookplate
Fly leaf

A Table of all ye Services contained in ys Book	1
f.1v blank	
A table of all ye Anthems contained in ys Book	2-4
f.4v blank	
Mr Tallis Short Service (1,2,4,6,7,8,10)	5-6
Mr Strogers Short Service (1,2,4,6,7,8,10)	6v-8
Mr Birds Short Service (1,2,4,6,7,8,10)	8-9v
Mr Thos Tomkins Short Service (1,2,4,6,7,8)	10-11v
Mr Bevins Short Service (1,2,4,6,7,8,10)	11v-14
The Nunc Dimittis of Mr Thomas Tomkins's Service in C fa ut (This disturbs the continuity of Bevins's Service)	12-12v
Mr Orlando Gibbons Short Service (1,2,4,6,7,8,10)	14-15v
Mr Albertus Brynes Short Service (2,5,6,7,8,10)	15v-16v
Mr Ben Rogers Short Sharp Service D Sharp (2,5,6,7,8,10)	16v-18
Behold now, praise the Lord (Benjamin Rogers) at the close of this item: 'The end of Mr Rogers short sharp service'	18
Dr Childs Service in D sol re sharp (2,5,6,7,8,10)	18v-20v
Dr Childes Service in E minor (2,5,6,7,8,10)	20v-22
Dr Childes Service in F (2,5,6,7,9,11)	23-24
Mr Richard Farrants high Service (2,4,6,7,8,10)	24-26
Mr Portmans Service (2,4,6,7,8,10)	26-27
Mr Thomas Tomkins Service in D sol re (2,5,6,7,8,10)	27v-28
Mr William Mundy's Service of 5 Parts 2 Contratenors (1,2,4,6,7,8,10)	28v-31
Dr Rogers's Service in Gamut (2,5,6,7,8,10)	31v-32
Mr Pellam Humfreys Service in E minor (2,5,6,7,8,10)	32v-33
Mr John Farrants Short Service (2,5,8,10)	33v-34
Mr Battens Short Service (2,5,6,7,8,10)	34v-35
Dr Rogers's Service in E la mi (2,5,6,7,8,10)	35v-36v
Mr Blows Short Service in G (2,5,8,10)	36v-37
Mr Patricks Service (2,4,8,10)	37-38

Dr Childs Benedicite Service (3,5,6,7,8,10)		38-38bis v
*Out of the deep	Henry Aldrich	38bis v
'Full Anthems' (heading)		38v
Almighty God, we beseech thee, give ear	Thos Heardson	38v
O Lord, give thy holy spirit	Thomas Tallis	38v
O God, be merciful unto us	Nicholas Strogers	38v-39
Call to remembrance	Mr Richard Farrant	39
Keep, we beseech thee, O good Lord	Thos Heardson	39
Hide not thou thy face	Richard Farrant	39v
I will exalt thee (with 2nd part, 'Sing unto the Lord')	Dr Tye	39v-40
O Lord, the maker of all thing	Mr William Mundy	40
O Lord, the world's Saviour	(William Mundy)	40-40v
Teach me thy way	Edmund Hooper	40v
Almighty and everlasting God	Orlando Gibbons	40v
O praise the Lord, all ye heathen	Adrian Batten	40v-41
Deliver us, O Lord (with 2nd part,'Blessed be the Lord God')	Orlando Gibbons	41
Hide not thou thy face	Adrian Batten	41
Lord, we beseech thee give ear	Adrian Batten	41v
Haste thee, O God (with 2nd part,'But let all those that seek thee')	Adrian Batten	41v
When the Lord turned again the captivity	Adrian Batten	41v
O God, whose neverfailing providence	Andrew Hecht	42
Blow out the trumpet	(Martin Peersons)	42
Zadok the priest	Henry Lawes	42
I give you a new commandment	John Cutts	42v
Sing, O daughter of Zion	Wilm Turner	42v
Mr Willm Tuckers Benedicite Service (3,5,6,7,8,10)		42v-43
Mr Willm Tuckers Short Service (2,5,8,10)		44-44v
O give thanks (Ps. 105)	Wilm Tucker	44v
'Anthems for 4 voyces' (heading)		45
Praise the Lord, O my soul (Ps. 103)	Dr Child	45

My soul truly waiteth	Adrian Batten	45
Deliver us, O Lord	Adrian Batten	45
O sing joyfully	Adrian Batten	45v
O clap your hands	Dr Child	45v
O Lord, grant the king a long life	Dr Child	45v-46
If the Lord himself	Dr Child	46
O pray for the peace of Jerusalem	Dr Willm Child	46-46v
Mr John Amners Service called Caesar's (2,5,6,7,8,10)		46v-48
O come hither, and hearken	John Amner	48
Mr John Amners Service of 4 parts (2,4,6,7,8,10)		48v-50
Mr Patricks Commandments & Creed		50
Mr John Blows Service in A re (2,5,6,7,9,11)		50v-51v
Mr Michael Wises Morning & Evening Service in D Minor (2,5,8,10)		51v-52
Dr Childs Service in A re (i.e. A minor) (2,5,6,7,8,10)		52-53
Dr Childs flatt Service in E la mi(2,5,6,7,8,10)		53-53v
Dr Childs Te Deum to his Benedicite, or his Service in Gamut (2,9,11)		54-54v
Mr Blows Benedicite Service or in E minor (3,5,6,7,9,11)		54v-56v
The Commandments & Creed to Mr Blows Service in G		56v
The Commandments and Creed to Mr Wises Service in D minor		56v-57
Mr Wises Commandments & Creed in E sharp (i.e., E major)		57
Dr Blows Te Deum in E minor		57-57v
Mr John Ferabosco's Evening Service for Verses in D sol re sharp (8,10)		57v-58
Mr Aldridg's Service in E la mi (3,5,6,7,8,10)		58-58v
& his Service in Gamut (2,5,6,7,8,10)		58v-59
A Second Creed (in triple time with Resp. to Commandments) in G of Dr Blows		59v
Mr Daniel Henstridgs Service with verses (2,5,6,7,8,10)		59v-60v
*Mr Purcel's Te Deum etc. in B flat (2,5,6,7,8,10)		60v-61v
'Anthems of 4 Parts' (heading)		62
Teach me,O Lord	Dr Rogers	62

Let my complaint come before thee	Adrian Batten	62-62v
O Lord God of hosts	Willm Turner	62
The Lord hear thee	John Blow	62v
O God, the king of glory	Henry Pursel	62v-63
Dr Blow's Te Deum to his Benedicite Service in E la mi		63-63v
f.64/64v blank		
'Full Anthems of 5 Parts' (heading)		65
With all our hearts	Thos Tallis	65
Blessed be thy name, O God	Thos Tallis	65
O thou God, Almighty Father	Edmund Hooper	65
I call and cry	Thos Tallis	65-65v
O Lord, I bow the knees of my heart	William Mundy	65
Prevent us, O Lord	Willm Bird	65v-66
Behold, it is Christ	Edmund Hooper	66
O Lord, make thy servant Charles	Willm Bird	66
I lift my heart to thee	Dr Tye	66v
O Lord, turn thy wrath (with 2nd part, 'Bow thine ear')	Willm Bird	66v-67
O give thanks	Dr Giles	67
O come let us sing unto the Lord	Robert Ramsey	67v
Why art thou so full of heaviness?	Thomas Wilkinson	67v
O Jerusalem, thou that killest the prophets	Thomas Wilkinson	67v-68
Almighty God, the fountain of all wisdom	Thomas Tomkins	68
Save me, O God (Ps. 54)	(William Birds)	68v
The Lord bless us	Willm White	68v
We beseech thee, Almighty God	Adrian Batten	69
O give thanks unto the Lord (Ps. 105)	Willm Tucker	69
O clap your hands	William Tucker	69v
I will sing unto the Lord	Henry Pursell	69v-70
O Lord, I have loved the habitation	Thos Tomkins	70

O God, wherefore art thou absent?	Will Turner (recte John Blow)	70
The king shall rejoice	John Tomkins	70-70v
Save me, O God (Ps. 69)	Mr Blow	70v
Save me, O God (Ps. 54)	Henry Pursell	70v-71
*O give thanks ...and his mercy	Dr Aldrige	71
*Have pity upon me, o ye my friends	Mr Wise	71-71v
*I beheld, and lo! a great multitude	Dr Rogers	71v-72
*Blessed is the man (Ps.1)	(Mr Sargenson)	72
*O praise the Lord (Ps. 135)	Dr Child	72v
*Service in A minor (8,10)	Dr Rogers	72v-73
*I waited patiently	John Blow	73-74
'Anthems for 6 & for more Parts' (heading)		74v
O praise God in his holiness	Willm White	74v
*O praise the Lord (Ps. 135)	(Dr Child)	74v
Deliver me from mine enemies	Robt Parsons	75
Sing joyfully	Willm Bird	75
*O sing unto the Lord (Ps. 98) (ending only)	William Child	75
Hosanna to the Son of David	Orlando Gibbons	75v
Lift up your heads	Orlando Gibbons	75v-76
O Clap your hands	Adrian Batten	76
Lord, who shall dwell in thy tabernacle?	Adrian Batten	76
God is our hope and strength (a 8)	Mr John Blow	76v
O clap your hands ('Dr Hethers Commencement Song') (with 2nd part,'God is gone up')	Mr Orlando Gibbons	76v-77
Inclina Domine	(Mr Ramsys)	77-77v
*Prepare ye the way ('2nd Treble in T.C.book')	Mr Wise	77v
*O sing unto the Lord (Ps. 98) (ending on f.75)	Dr Child	78
*O praise God in his holiness	(Mr Wise)	78-78v
*O clap your hands ('2nd Treble in T.C.book')	Dr Rogers	78v

*The Lord said unto my Lord ('2nd Treble in T.C.book')	Mr Wise	79
*Thy way, O God, is holy	Mr Purcell	79
Blessed be the Lord my strength	Henry Purcell	79v
Hear, O heavens	Mr Pellam Humfrys	79v
O how amiable are thy dwellings	John Blow	79v
Lord, thou hast been our refuge	William Turner	79v
Behold, God is my salvation	Thomas Tudway	79v-80
Lord, teach us to number our days	Mr Pelham Humfrys	80
O give thanks (Ps. 118)	Mr Pellham Humfrys	80-81
Like as the hart	Mr Pellham Humfry	80v
O Lord, thou hast searched me out	Mr John Blow	80v-81
*Behold now, praise the Lord	(Dr Blows)	81
*Hear my prayer, O Lord (Ps.102)	Mr Turner	81
*I will sing a new song	Mr Wise	81v
*I will alway give thanks	Pelham Humfrey, John Blow, William Turner	81v
*O give thanks (Ps.106)	Henry Purcell	82
*Teach me, O Lord	Dr Christopher Gibbons	82v
'A Collection of such Anthems for verses as have bin made at Lincoln in ye years 68, 69 & 70'		
(heading)		83
O praise the Lord (Ps.147)	Willm Turner	83
Hear my crying, O God	Andreas Hecht	83
By the waters of Babylon	John Cutts	83
Praise the Lord, ye servants	Andreas Hecht	83-83v
Comfort ye, my people	Willm Tucker	83v
Sing unto the Lord, O ye kingdoms	Willm Turner	83v
The earth is the Lord's	Willm Turner	83v-84
This is the day	Willm Turner	84
O be joyful in God	Willm Turner	84
Blessed is the man (Ps.1)	Andreas Hecht	84
Praise the Lord, O my soul (Ps.103)	Andreas Hecht	84v

How long wilt thou forget me?	Albertus Bryne	92-92v
How long wilt thou forget me?	Dr Christopher Gibbons	92v-93
My beloved spake(Note: 'Thus in ye printed book')	Thos Tomkins	93
Thou are my king, O God	Thos Tomkins	93-93v
O Lord, make thy servant Charles	Willm Cranford	93v
My song shall be of mercy	Henry Lawes	93v
Now that the Lord hath re-advanced the crown	William King	93v-94
Let all the world in every corner sing	Henry Loosemore	94
O how amiable are thy dwellings	Mr Loe (Edward Lowe)	94-94v
O how happy a thing it is	Adrian Batten	94v
Bow down thine ear	John Ward	94v
I will magnify thee	(John Wards)	94v-95
O Lord our governor	Adrian Batten	95
Unto thee, O Lord, do I lift up	Will Tucker	95-95v
Above the stars my saviour dwells	Dr Christopher Gibbons	95v-96
Behold, I bring you glad tidings	Ben Rogers	96-96v
O give thanks (Ps.107)	Ben Rogers	96v
O that mine eyes would melt	George Loosemore	96v-97
Hear my prayer, O Lord, and let thine ear	Thomas Wilkinson	97-97v
Preserve me, O Lord (concluded on f.98v)	Thos Wilkinson	97v-98
Let God arise	(John Wards)	98
The Lord is my light	Willm Lawes	98-98v
Hear my crying, O God	Andreas Hecht	98v-100
I will give thanks (Ps.138)	John Cutts	100
Comfort ye, my people	Wilm Tucker	100-100v
O come hither and hearken	(John Cutts)	100v
Praise the Lord, ye servants	Willm Tucker	100v-101

O praise the Lord, all ye heathen	Dr Christopher Gibbons	108-108v
Rejoice in the Lord, O ye righteous	Richard Portman	108v
Not unto us	Matthew Lock	108v
My God, my God, look upon me ('Organist of Kings Colledge in Cambridge')	Thos Tudway	109
This is the day	Willm Tucker	109-109v
O Lord our governor	Henry Pursell	109v-110
Have mercy upon me	Pellham Humfrys	110
O Lord, I have sinned	Mr Blows	110-110v
Christ being raised	Mr John Blow	110v
God be merciful unto us	Dr Christopher Gibbons	110v-111
Let God arise	Henry Pursel	111
Behold, how good and joyful a thing	Dr Childs	111
Lord, I am not high minded	Dr Christopher Gibbons's	111v
Let God arise	Dr Child	111v
Sing unto the Lord, O ye saints	Dr Christopher Gibbons	112
Out of the deep	Willm Grigory	112
God be merciful unto us	John Blow	112v
Thou art my king, O God	Dr Child	112v
O God, thou hast cast us out	Willm Grigory	113
Awake, put on thy strength	Michael Wise	113
Mr Pursel's chorus to his Anthem O praise the Lord, all ye heathen		113
*I was glad	Mr Pursel	113
*Try me, O God	Dr Turner	113v
*O God, to whom vengeance belongeth	Anonimous J.B. (recte John Blow?)	113v
*When the Son of Man shall come	Dr Blow	113v
*God is our hope and strength	(Dr Aldrich)	114
*Hide not thou thy face	R.Farrant, adapted by Henry Aldrich	114-114v

*Give sentence with me   (Dr Aldrich) based on 114v
O.Gibbons,'Almighty and
everlasting God'

Inside back cover: Eight Psalm Tunes (Single Chants):

William Child	F
John Blow	E minor
'T.P.'	G minor (Zimmerman, D.33
'E.P.	D minor (Zimmerman, Z.123)
William Turner	A
	D
	B minor
Pelham Humfrey	C (the 'Grand Chant')

(2) Contratenor Decani

Inside front cover: 'W.Gostling' and bookplate

Fly-leaf, containing (i) some indecipherable pencil note;
(ii) in Bing's hand:
Begotten of his see if ye crotchet be in D & E
or in C & D in ye Contratenor of Childs service
in D sharp.

Mr John Amners Caesars Service of 5 parts
  (2,5,6,7,8,10)   38v-40

O come hither, and hearken   John Amner   40
  ('The Anthem to the Service')

Mr Patricks Kyrie & Creed   40v

Mr Blows Service in A re (2,5,6,7,9,11)   40v-41v

Mr Michael Wises Morning & Evening Service
  in D minor (2,5,8,10)   41v

Dr Childs Service in A re (i.e.A minor)
  (2,5,6,7,8,10)   42-43

Dr Childs Flatt Service in E (2,5,6,7,8,10)   43-43v

Dr Childs Te Deum to his Benedicite Service   43v-44

Dr Childs Evening Service in Gamut (9,11)   44-44v

The Commandments & Creed to Mr Blows Service in G   44v-45

Dr Child's Service in E la mi sharp (i.e. E minor)
  as it is on Cantoris Side (2,5,6,7,8,10)   45-45v

Mr Wises Commandments & Creed in E la mi Sharp
  (i.e., E major)   46

Dr Blows Te Deum to his Benedicite Service
  (incomplete)   46v

Mr Alldrigs Service in E la mi (3,5,6,7,8,10)   46v-47v

Mr Ferabosco's Evening Service for Verses (8,10)   47v

Mr Aldrigs Service in Gamut (2,5,6,7,8,10)   47v-48v

Dr Blows 2nd Creed in G (triple time) (6,7)   48v

*Mr Purcells Service in B flat (2,4,6,7,8,10)   48v-49v

f.50 blank

'Full Anthems of 4 Parts' (heading)   51

Almighty God, we beseech thee   Thos Heardson   51

O Lord, give thy holy spirit   Thos Tallis   51

O God, be merciful   Nicholas Strogers 51

Call to remembrance   Richard Farrant   51v

Keep, we beseech thee,
  O good Lord   Mr Heardson   51v

Hide not thou thy face   Richard Farrant   51v

I will exalt thee (with 2nd
  part,'Sing unto the Lord')   Dr Tye   51v-52

O Lord, the maker of all thing   Willm Mundy   52

O Lord, the world's saviour   Willm Mundy   52v

Teach me thy way   Edmund Hooper   52v

Almighty and everlasting God   Orlando Gibbons   52v

38

We beseech thee, Almighty God	Adrian Batten	70v
Lord, who shall dwell in thy tabernacle?	Adrian Batten	70v
Hear my prayer, O God	Adrian Batten	70v-71
O give thanks (Ps.105)	Willm Tucker	71
O clap your hands	Adrian Batten	71-71v
The Lord bless us and keep us ('This Anthem is to be put on Cantoris side')	Willm White	71v
Turn thy face from my sins	Matthew Lock	71v-72
I will sing unto the Lord	Henry Pursell	72
O clap your hands	Willm Tucker	72-72v
O Lord God of hosts	Willm Turner	72v
O Lord, I have loved the habitation	Thos Tomkins	73
Save me, O God (Ps.54)	Henry Pursel	73
*Hear my prayer, O Lord (Ps.102)	Mr Turner	73
*Praise the Lord, O my soul (Ps.146)	Mr Loosmore	73v
*Have pity upon me, O ye my friends	Mr Wise	73v
*Hear my prayer, O Lord (Ps.102)	Mr Turner	74
Mr Robert Ramsy's Commencement Song of 8 Parts Inclina Domine		74v
Dr Hethers Commencement Song composed by Mr Orlando Gibbons O clap your hands		75
'Anthems of 6 or more Parts' (heading)		75v
Sing joyfully unto God	Will Bird	75v
Deliver me from mine enemies	Robert Parsons	75v
Hosanna to the Son of David	Orlando Gibbons	76
Lift up your heads (note:'Batten, Lord who shall dwell & O clap your hands are among ye 5 parts')	Orlando Gibbons	76
The king shall rejoice	Joh Tomkins	76v
O God, wherefore art thou absent?	Mr Blow	76v
God is our hope and strength (a 8)	Mr Blow	76v-77
Save me, O God (Ps.69)	Mr Blow	77

O praise God in his holiness	Willm White	77
Holy, holy, holy	Adrian Batten	77v
Unto thee, O Lord	Richard Deering	77v
Behold, God is my salvation	Mr Tedway	78
I will praise the Lord (completion at foot of f.77v)	(Mr Wards)	78
Praise the Lord ye servants	Andrew Hecht	78v
Lord, I am not high minded	Dr Christopher Gibbons	78v
'Anthems for Verses' (heading)		79
Almighty God, who by the leading of a star	Dr Bull	79
In thee, O Lord, put I my trust	Dr Bull	79
Behold, thou hast made my days	Orlando Gibbons	79v
Blessed are all they	Orlando Gibbons	79v
Behold, I bring you glad tidings	Orlando Gibbons	79v-80
Glorious and powerful God	Orlando Gibbons	80-80v
If ye be risen again with Christ	Orlando Gibbons	80v
Out of the deep	Thos Morley	80v-81
How long wilt thou forget me?	Thos Morley	81
O Lord, let me know mine end	Thos Tomkins	81-81v
Let God arise	John Ward	81v-82
Thou art my King, O God	Thos Tomkins	82
O Lord, make thy servant Charles	Willm Cranford	82-82v
I heard a voice from heaven saying, Allelujah	Albertus Bryne	82v
O praise God in his holiness	Edward Smith	82v-83
Hear my prayer, O Lord, and let thine ear	Thos Wilkinson	83
My song shall be of mercy	Henry Laws	83
Now that the Lord hath readvanced the crown	William King	83-83v

Lord, who shall dwell in thy tabernacle?	Andreas Hecht	92-92v
The Lord is my light	Willm Laws	92v
Lord, who shall dwell in thy tabernacle?	Mr Portmans	92v-93
Blessed is the man (Ps.1)	Mr Wise	93
Lord, what is man?	Wilm Turner	93-93v
Lord, let me know mine end	(Matthew Lockes)	93v-94
O give thanks (Ps.107)	Willm Tucker	94
Wherewithal shall a young man cleanse his ways?	Willm Tucker	94-94v
Lord, how are they increased	John Blow	94v
Behold, how good and joyful a thing	John Blow	94v
Awake up my glory	Michael Wise	94v-95
I will cry unto thee, O God	John Blow	95
God standeth in the congregation	Henry Hall	95
How are the mighty fallen	Michael Wise	95v
Turn thee unto me	John Blow	95v
Rejoice in the Lord, O ye righteous	Pelham Humfry	95v
I will magnify thee	Will Tucker	96
I was glad	William Tucker	96-96v
By the waters of Babylon	Michael Wise	96v-97
Christ being raised from the dead	John Blow	97
Blessed is he that considereth the poor	Michael Wise	97-97v
O Lord, thou hast searched me out	Mr Blow	97v
Rejoice in the Lord, O ye righteous	Richard Portman	97v
Not unto us	Mr Lock	98
My God, my God, look upon me ('Organist of King's College in Cambridge')	Thos Tudway	98-98v
This is the day	Will Tucker	98v
Lord, how long wilt thou be angry?	Willm Tucker	99
O be joyful in the Lord	Pelham Humfrys	99

Haste thee, O God	Pelham Humfrys	99-99v
The earth is the Lord's	Dr Child	99v
Turn thee unto me	John Blow	99v-100
O Lord our governor	Henry Pursell	100
I am well pleased	William Tucker	100v
My heart is fixed	Willm Tucker	100v
Sing we merrily	John Blow	100v-101
I will alway give thanks	Pelham Humfrys, Joh Blow, Willm Turner	101
Comfort ye, my people	Will Tucker	101
O praise the Lord, all ye heathen	Dr Christopher Gibbons	101v
The Lord said unto my Lord	(Dr Christopher Gibbons)	101v
Praise the Lord, ye servants	Will Tucker	101v
Have mercy upon me	Pelham Humfrys	101v-102
O Lord, I have sinned	John Blow	102-102v
Christ being raised from the dead	John Blow	102v
By the waters of Babylon	Henry Hall	102v
By the waters of Babylon	Mr Pelham Humfrys	103
Not unto us	(Matthew Lock)	103-103v
Let God arise	Mr Willm Laws	103v
Blow up the trumpet	Henry Pursel	103v-104
Let God arise	Henry Pursel	104-104v
O how amiable are thy dwellings	Mr John Blow	104v
Like as the hart	Pelham Humfrey	105
God be merciful unto us	Dr Christopher Gibbons	105
Blessed be the Lord my strength	Henry Purcell	105-105v
Hear, O heavens	Pelham Humfrey	105v
Lord, thou hast been our refuge	William Turner	105v-106
Lord, teach us to number	Mr Pelham Humfrys	106
O give thanks (Ps.118) ('This in Westminster books is on Cantoris Side & ye Verses are on yt side'.)	Pelham Humfrey	106-106v
O Lord my God	Pelham Humfrys	106v

Let God arise	Dr Child	107
Sing unto the Lord, O ye saints	Dr Christopher Gibbons	107
Out of the deep	Willm Grigory	107-107v
God be merciful unto us	John Blow	107v
Thou art my King, O God	Dr Child	107v
O God, thou hast cast us out	Willm Gregory	107v
Behold, how good and joyful a thing	Dr Child	107v-108
Awake, awake, put on thy strength	Michael Wise	108
O praise the Lord, all ye heathen	Henry Pursel	108
*Prepare ye the way	Mr Wise	108v
*O sing unto the Lord (Ps.98)	Dr Child	108v
*O praise God in his holiness	Mr Wise	108v

Inside back cover: Eight Psalm Tunes (as for Medius Decani)

(3) Tenor Decani

Inside front cover: 'W.Gostling' and bookplate
ff. 1 - 4 blank
A Table of all ye Services & Anthems contained
  in this Book   5-6

A Book of Services and Anthems for a Quire   6v

Mr Tallis's short Service (1,2,4,6,7,8,10)   7-8v

Mr Strogers short Service (1,2,4,6,7,8,10)   8v-10v

Mr Birds short Service (1,2,4,6,7,8,10)   10v-12

Mr Thomas Tomkins's short Service (1,2,4,6,7,8,10) 12v-14

Mr Bevin short Service (1,2,4,6,7,8,10)   14-15v

Mr Orlando Gibbons's short Service (1,2,4,6,7,8,10) 15v-17

Mr Brynes short Service (2,5,6,7,8,10)   17-18

Mr Ben Rogers short sharp Service (2,5,6,7,8,10) 18v-19v

Behold now, praise the Lord   Benjamin Rogers 19v

Dr Childes sharp Service in D sol re
  (2,5,6,7,8,10)   19v-21

Dr Childes Service in E minor (2,5,6,7,8,10)   21-22

& allso Child's Service in F (2,5,6,7,9,11)   22-23v

Mr Richard Farrants high Service (2,4,6,7,8,10)   23v-25

Mr Portmans Service (2,4,6,7,8,10)   25-26v

Mr Thomas Tomkins's Service in D minor
  (2,5,6,7,8,10)   26v-28v

Mr Reads Evening Service (8,10)   28v-29

Mr Mundy's Service of 5. parts (1,2,4,6,7,8,10)   29-31v

Dr Rogers's Service in Gamut (2,4,6,7,8,10)   32-33

Mr Pellham Humfreys short Service in E la mi
  (2,5,6,7,8,10)   33v-34v

Mr John Farrants short Service (2,5,6,7,8,10)   34v-35

Mr Adrian Battens short Service (2,5,6,7,8,10)   35-36

Dr Rogers's Service in E la mi (2,5,6,7,8,10)   36-37

Mr Blows short Service in G (2,5,8,10)   37-37v

Mr Patricks short Service (2,4,6,8,10)   38-38v

Dr Childs Benedicite Service (3,5,6,7,8,10)   38v-39v

Mr Tuckers Benedicite Service (3,5,6,7,8,10)   39v-40v

John Amners Caesar's Service (2,5,6,7,8,10)   40v-42v

O come hither, and hearken   John Amner 42v

Mr John Amner's Service of 4 parts (2,4,6,7,8,10) 42v-44

Mr Patricks Kiery & Creed (for Cantoris side) (6,7) 44-44v

Mr Blows Service in A re (2,5,6,7,9,11)   44v-45v

Mr Wises Morning & Evening Service in D minor   45v-46
  (2,5,6,8,10)

Dr Childs Service in A re (i.e., A minor)   46-46v
  (2,5,6,7,8,10)

Dr Childs Te Deum to his Benedicite Service
  in Gamut (2)   47

Dr Childs verse Evening Service (9)   47

The Commandments & Creed of Mr Blows Service in G   47v

This following belongs to ye next foregoing
  Service of Dr Childs (11)   47v

Mr John Blow's Service in E minor or his
  Benedicite Service (3,5,6,7,9,11)   48-49v

& his (John Blow's) Second Commandments
  & Creed in G   49v

'Full Anthems of 4 parts' (heading)   50

Almighty God, we beseech thee,
  give ear   Thos Heardson   50

O Lord, give thy holy spirit   Thos Tallis   50

O God, be merciful unto us   Nicholas Strogers   50

Call to remembrance   Richard Farrant   50v

Keep, we beseech thee,
  O good Lord   Thos Heardson   50v

Hide not thou thy face   Richard Farrant   50v

I will exalt thee (with 2nd
  part,'Sing unto the Lord')   Dr Tye   50v-51

O Lord, the maker of all thing   Wm Mundy   51

O Lord, the world's Saviour   Willm Mundy   51v

Teach me thy way   Edmund Hooper   51v

Almighty and everlasting God   Orlando Gibbons   51v-52

O praise the Lord, all ye
  heathen   Adrian Batten   52

Deliver us, O Lord our God
  (with 2nd part,'Blessed be
  the Lord God of Israel')   Orlando Gibbons   52

Hide not thou thy face   Adrian Batten   52-52v

Lord, we beseech thee
  give ear   Adrian Batten   52v

Haste thee, O God (with 2nd
  part,'But let all those
  that seek')   Adrian Batten   52v

When the Lord turned again the captivity	Adrian Batten	52v
O God, whose never failing providence	Andreas Hecht	53
Blow out the trumpet	Martin Peerson	53
I give you a new commandment	John Cutts	53
Behold, how good and joyful a thing	Willm Turner	53v
Sing, O daughter of Zion	Willm Turner	53v
O give thanks (Ps.107)	Dr Rogers's	53v-54
Let thy merciful ears	John Cutts	54
My soul truly waiteth	Mr Batten	54
Deliver us, O Lord	Adrian Batten	54
O sing joyfully	Adrian Batten	54v
O clap your hands	Dr Wm Child	54v
O pray for the peace of Jerusalem	Dr Wm Child	54v
O Lord, grant the king a long life	William Child	55
If the Lord himself	William Child	55
O give thanks (Ps.105)	Willm Tucker	55v
Praise the Lord, O my soul (Ps.103)	Dr Child	55v
Teach me, O Lord	Dr Rogers	56
O God, the King of glory	Henry Pursel	56
The Lord hear thee	Mr John Blow	56-56v
Let my complaint come before thee	Adrian Batten	56v
O Lord God of hosts	Willm Turner	56v
'Full Anthems of 5 parts' (heading)		57
With all our hearts	Thos Tallis	57
Blessed be thy name, O God	Thos Tallis	57
O thou God, Almighty Father	Edmund Hooper	57
O Lord, I bow the knees of my heart	Wm Mundy	57-57v
I call and cry	Thos Tallis	57v
Pevent us, O Lord	Willm Bird	57v-58
Behold, it is Christ	Edmund Hooper	58
O Lord, make thy servant Charles	Willm Bird	58

I lift my heart to thee	Dr Tye	58v
O Lord, turn thy wrath (with 2nd part,'Bow thine ear')	Willm Bird	58v-59
O give thanks	Dr Giles	59
O come, let us sing unto the Lord	Robert Ramsey	59v
Why art thou so full of heaviness?	Thos Wilkinson	59v
O Jerusalem, thou that killest the prophets	Thos Wilkinson	59v-60
Almighty God, the fountain of all wisdom	Thos Tomkins	60
Hear my prayer, O God	Adrian Batten	60-60v
We beseech thee, Almighty God	Adrian Batten	60v
The Lord bless us	Willm White	60v-61
O clap your hands	Willm Tucker	61
I will sing unto the Lord	Henry Pursell	61-61v
Save me, O God (Ps.69)	John Blow	61v
Save me, O God (Ps.54)	Henry Pursel	61v
*Mr Purcells Service in B flat (2,4,6,7,8,10)		62
'Anthems of 6 & 7 parts' (heading)		63
Deliver me from mine enemies	Robert Parsons	63
Sing joyfully	Willm Bird	63
Lord, who shall dwell in thy tabernacle?	Adrian Batten	63-63v
O clap your hands	Adrian Batten	63v
Hosanna to the Son of David	Orlando Gibbons	63v-64
Lift up your heads	Orlando Gibbons	64
The King shall rejoice	John Tomkins	64-64v
O clap your hands (Dr Heathers commencement Song composed by Orlando Gibbons)		64v
Inclina Domine (Mr Robert Ramsys Commencement Song of 8 pts)		65
O praise God in his holiness	Willm White	65v
*Blessed is the man (Ps.1)	John Sargenson	65v-66
*Try me, O God	Dr Turner	66
ff. 66v, 67 blank		

Lord, I am not high minded	Dr Christopher Gibbons's	68
*Praise the Lord, O my soul (Ps.146)	Henry Loosemore	68
Unto thee, O Lord, will I lift up	Richard Deering	68v
God is our hope and strength	John Blow	68v
Holy, holy, holy	Mr Baten	68v
O God, whose never failing providence	Andreas Hecht	69
In thee, O Lord, do I put my trust	Dr Bull	69
Save me, O God (Ps.54)	Willm Bird	69
Unto thee, O Lord, do I lift up	Willm Tucker	69v
O be joyful in God	Willm Turner	69v
Behold, I bring you good tidings	Ben Rogers	70
Sing unto the Lord, O ye kingdoms	Willm Turner	70
This is the day	W. Turner	70-70v
Praise the Lord, O my soul (Ps.103)	Andreas Hecht	70v
Above the stars the Saviour dwells	Dr Christopher Gibbons	70v-71
My days are gone	John Cutts	71
O praise the Lord, ye angels	John Cutts	71
O sing unto the Lord (Ps.98)	John Cutts	71
O praise the Lord (Ps.147)	Wilm Turner	71v
Hear my crying, O God	Andreas Hecht	71v
By the waters of Babylon	John Cutts	71v
Praise the Lord, ye servants	Andreas Hecht	71v-72
Comfort ye, my people	Wilm Tucker	72
Lord, who shall dwell in thy tabernacle?	Andreas Hecht	72
Haste thee, O God	Andreas Hecht	72
Look, shepherds, look	Unattributed	72v-73
Behold, I bring you glad tidings	Orlando Gibbons	73

I heard a voice in heaven saying, Allelujah	Albertus Bryne	73-73v
O that mine eyes would melt	George Loosmore	73v
Blessed is the man (Ps.1)	Andreas Hecht	74
Almighty God, which by the leading of a star	Dr Bull	74v
Out of the deep	Thomas Morley	74v
Behold, thou hast made my days	Orlando Gibbons	75
Blessed are all they	Orlando Gibbons	75v
O Lord, let me know mine end	Thos Tomkins	75v-76
O Lord, make thy servant Charles	Willm Cranford	76-76v
Bow down thine ear	John Ward	76v-77
I will magnify thee	John Cutts	77
My song shall be of mercy	Henry Lawes	77v
Now that the Lord hath readvanced the crown	William King	78
Out of the deep	Adrian Batten	78-78v
Glorious and powerful God	Orlando Gibbons	78v
Thou art my King, O God	Thos tomkins	79
O Lord our governor	Adrian Batten	79-79v
My beloved spake	Thos tomkins	79v-80
I will praise the Lord	John Ward	80-80v
O how amiable are thy dwellings	Mr Loe	80v
How long wilt thou forget me?	Albert Bryne	80v-81
Let God arise	John Ward	81-81v
O praise God in his holiness	Edward Smith	81v
O how happy a thing it is	Adrian Batten	82
Let all the world in every corner sing	Henry Loosmore	82
Preserve me, O Lord	Thos Wilkinson	82-82v
Hear my prayer, O Lord, and let thine ear	Thos Wilkinson	82v
Save me, O God (Ps.54)	Willm Bird	82v-83
Zadok the priest	Henry Lawes	83
How long wilt thou forget me?	Dr Christopher Gibbons	83
If ye be risen again	Orlando Gibbons	83
How long wilt thou forget me?	Mr Morley	83v
The earth is the Lord's	Willm Turner	83v

Christ rising again	Mr Batten	84
By the waters of Babylon	Willm Turner	84-84v
I will give thanks (Ps.138)	John Cutts	84v
O sing unto the Lord (Ps.149)	Willm King	84v
The Lord is my light	Willm Lawes	85
O come hither, and hearken	John Cutts	85
Lord, how long wilt thou be angry?	Willm Tucker	85v
Praise the Lord, ye servants	William Tucker	85v
Lord, who shall dwell in thy tabernacle?	Mr Portmans	86
Blessed is the man (Ps.1)	(Michael Wise)	86-86v
Lord, what is man?	Willm Turner	86v
Lord, let me know mine end	(Mr Lock)	86v-87
Turn thy face from my sins	Matthew Locke	87-87v
O give thanks (Ps. 107)	Willm Tucker	87v
Lord, how are they increased	John Blow	87v-88
Wherewithal shall a young man mend his ways?	Will Tucker	88
Behold, how good and joyful a thing	John Blow	88-88v
Awake up, my glory	Michael Wise	88v
God standeth in the congregation	Henry Hall	88v
I will cry unto thee, O God	(John Blow)	88v-89
How are the mighty fallen	Michael Wise	89-89v
Turn thee unto me	John Blow	89v
Rejoice in the Lord, O ye righteous	Pellham Humfreys	89v-90
I will magnify thee	Will Tucker	90-90v
I was glad	Will Tucker	90v
By the waters of Babylon	Michael Wise	90v
Christ being raised from the dead	John Blow	90v-91
Blessed is he that considereth the poor	Michael Wise	91
The Lord said unto my Lord	(Dr Christopher Gibbons)	91

O Lord, thou hast searched me out	John Blow	91v
Rejoice in the Lord, O ye righteous	Richard Portman	91v
Not unto us	Matthew Lock	91v-92
The earth is the Lord's	Dr Child	92
My God, my God, look upon me	Thos Tudway	92v-93
This is the day	Willm Tucker	93
Haste thee, O God	Pellham Humfreys	93-93v
I am well pleased	Willm Tucker	93v
O Lord our governor	Henry Pursel	93v-94
My heart is fixed	Willm Tucker	94
Sing we merrily	John Blow	94-94v
I will alway give thanks	Pelham Humfrey, William Turner, John Blow	94v
Haste thee, O God	Pelham Humfrey	94v-95
O praise the Lord, all ye heathen	Dr Christopher Gibbons	95
Have mercy upon me	Pelham Humfrys	95-95v
O Lord, I have sinned	John Blow	95v
Christ being raised from the dead	John Blow	95v-96
Behold, God is my salvation	Willm Turner	96-96v
By the waters of Babylon	Pellham Humfrys	96v
Not unto us	Matthew Lock	97
Let God arise	Willm Laws	97
Blow up the trumpet	Henry Pursell	97-97v
Let God arise	Henry Pursel	97v-98
Blessed be the Lord, my strength	Henry Pursel	98
Hear, O heavens	Mr Humfrys	98-98v
O how amiable are thy dwellings	Mr Blow	98v
Lord, thou hast been our refuge	Willm Turner	98v-99
Behold, God is my salvation	Mr Tudway	99
Lord, teach us to number our days	Mr Pellham Humfrys	99-99v

O give thanks (Ps.118)	Pelham Humfrys	99v
Like as the hart	Pellham Humfrys	99v-100
O God, wherefore art thou absent?	John Blow	100
God be merciful unto us	Dr Christopher Gibbons	100-100v
O Lord, rebuke me not	Dr Childs	100v
Behold, how good and joyful a thing	(Dr Child)	100v
O Lord my God	Mr Pellham Humfry	100v
Let God arise	Dr Child	100v
Out of the deep	Willm Grigory	101
God be merciful unto us	John Blow	101
Thou art my King, O God	Dr Child	101
O God, thou hast cast us out	Willm Grigory	101-101v
Awake, awake, put on thy strength	Michael Wise	101v-102
O praise the Lord, all ye heathen	Henry Pursel	102-102v

The Commandments & Creed of Mr Wises in D sol re to his Service page 78 (f.45v). It should be on Cantoris side.   102v

His (Michael Wise's) Commandments & Creed in E la mi sharp (i.e., in E major)	102v-103
Dr Blows Te Deum to his Service in E minor	103-103v
Mr Aldridgs Benedicite Service (3,5,6,7,8,10)	103v-104
Mr Ferabosco's Evening Service (8,10)	104-104v
Mr Aldridg's Service in Gamut (2,5,6,7,8,10)	104v-105

*Verse belonging to O give thanks (Ps.118)	Pelham Humfrey	105

ff.105v, 106 blank

Mr Tallis's Te Deum and Benedictus for both sides	107-107v
Dr Childs flatt Service in E (2,5,6,7,8,10)	107v-108
The Epiphany Anthem for me Tenor Decani as its in ye Westminster books (Almighty God, who by the leading of a star) John Bull	108v

ff.109-112 blank

Inside back cover: Eight Psalm Tunes (as for Medius Decani)

(4) Bass Decani

Inside front cover: Signature 'W.Gostling' and bookplate
Fly-leaf

Mr Patricks Kyrie & Creed		38-38v
Mr John Blows Service in A re (2,5,6,7,9,11)		38v-39v
Mr Wises Morning & Evening Service in D sol re (2,5,8,10)		39v-40
Dr Childs Service in A re (i.e., A minor) (2,5,6,7,8,10)		40-40v
Dr Childs Flatt Service in E (2,5,6,7,8,10)		40v-41
Dr Childs Te Deum to his Benedicite Service in Gamut & his Evening Service for verses in G (2,9,11)		41v-42
Mr John Blows Service in E minor or his Benedicite Service (3,5,6,7,9,11)		42-43v
The Creed to his (John Blow's) Service in G (6,7)		43v-44
Mr Wises Sharp Creed in E la mi (i.e.,E major) (6,7) & his in D sol re (6,7)		44-44v
Dr Blow's Te Deum to his Benedicite Service		44v-45
Mr Henry Aldridg's Benedicite Service in E la mi (3,5,6,7,8,10)		45-45v
Mr Joh Ferabosco's Evening Service for verses (8,10)		45v
Mr Aldridg's Service in Gamut (2,5,6,7,8,10)		45v-46
Dr Blow's Second Creed in Gamut (triple time) (6,7)		46v
*Mr Purcells service in B flat (2,4,6,7,8,10)		46v-48
*Dr Blow's Te Deum to his Service in E la mi		48
ff.48v, 49 blank		
'Full Anthems of 4 Parts' (heading)		50
Almighty God, we beseech thee, give ear	Thos Heardson	50
O Lord, give thy holy spirit	Thos Tallis	50
O God, be merciful unto us	Nicholas Strogers	50
Call to remembrance	Richard Farrant	50v
Keep, we beseech thee, O good Lord	Thomas Heardson	50v
Hide not thou thy face	(Mr Richard Farrant)	50v
I will exalt thee (with 2nd part,'Sing unto the Lord')	Dr Tye	50v-51
O Lord, the maker of all thing	Willm Mundy	51
O Lord, the world's saviour	Willm Mundy	51v
Teach me thy way	Richard Farrant (recte E.Hooper)	51v
Almighty and everlasting God	Orlando Gibbons	51v

*Out of the deep	Dr Aldrich	58v
*O praise the Lord (Ps.135)	Dr Child	58v-59
*O God, to whom vengeance belongeth	J sine nomine B (recte John Blow?)	59
ff.59v,60, 61, 62,63 blank		
'Full Anthems of 5 Parts' (heading)		64
With all our hearts	Thos Tallis	64
Blessed be thy name, O God	Thos Tallis	64
O thou God, Almighty Father	Edmund Hooper	64
I call and cry	Thos Tallis	64-64v
O Lord, I bow the knees of my heart	Willm Mundy	64v
Prevent us, O Lord	Willm Bird	64v-65
Behold, it is Christ	Edmund Hooper	65
O Lord, make thy servant Charles	(William Bird)	65
I lift my heart to thee ɘe	Dr Tye	65-65v
O Lord, turn thy wrath (with 2nd part,'Bow thine ear')	Willm Bird	65v
O give thanks	Dr Giles	65v-66
O come, let us sing unto the Lord	Robert Ramsey	66
O Jerusalem, thou that killest the prophets	Mr Wilkinson	66-66v
Why art thou so full of heaviness?	Mr Wilkinson	66v
Almighty God, the fountain of all wisdom	Thos Tomkins	66v
Save me, O God (Ps.54)	Willm Bird	67
Hear my prayer, O God	Adrian Batten	67
We beseech thee, Almighty God	Mr Batten	67-67v
Hear my prayer, O God	Adrian Batten	67v
O give thanks (Ps.105)	Will Tucker	67v-68
The Lord bless us	Willm White	68
O clap your hands	Willm Tucker	68
I will sing unto the Lord	Henry Pursell	68v
O Lord, I have loved the habitation	Thos Tomkins	68v

Save me, O God (Ps.54)	Henry Pursell	68v–69
*O praise God in his holiness	Mr Wise	69–69v
*O clap your hands	Dr Rogers	69v
*The Lord said unto my Lord	(Mr Wise)	69v–70
*Thy way, O God, is holy	Henry Purcell	70–70v
*I waited patiently	Dr Blow	71
*When the Son of Man shall come	Dr Blow	71–71v
*O be joyful in God	Dr Blow	71v–72
*Thy word is a lantern (incomplete)	Henry Purcell	72v
f.73 recto blank		
O praise God in his holiness	Mr White	73v
f.74 recto blank		
Mr Robert Ramsys Commencement Song of 8 Parts Inclina Domine		74v
Dr Heathers Commencement Song composed by Mr Orlando Gibbons, O clap your hands		75
The king shall rejoice	John Tompkins	75v
God is our hope and strength (a 8)	Mr John Blow	75v
'Full Anthems of 6 Parts' (heading)		
Sing joyfully	Willm Bird	76
Deliver me from mine enemies	Robert Parsons	76
Hosanna to the Son of David	Orlando Gibbons	76–76v
Lift up your heads	Orlando Gibbons	76v
O Lord, grant the king a long life	Thomas Weelks	76v
O clap your hands	Adrian Batten	76v–77
Lord, who shall dwell in thy tabernacle?	Adrian Batten	77
O Lord, thou hast searched me out	Adrian Batten	77–77v
Lord, let me know mine end	(Matthew Lock)	77v–78
My beloved spake	Thomas Tomkins	78
*Teach me, O Lord	Dr Christopher Gibbons	78
ff.78v, 79 blank		
Blessed is he that considereth the poor	Michael Wise	80

Out of the deep	Thos Morley	80v
Out of the deep	Adrian Batten	80v
I will praise the Lord	John Ward	80v-81
Holy, holy, holy	Adrian Batten	81
Unto thee, O Lord, will I lift up	Richard Deering	81
If ye be risen again with Christ	Orlando Gibbons	81v
Behold, I bring you glad tidings	Orlando Gibbons	81v
Glorious and powerful God	Orlando Gibbons	81v-82
Behold, God is my salvation	Willm Turner	82-82v
Haste thee, O God	Andrew Hecht	82v
Praise the Lord, ye servants	Andrew Hecht	83
Unto thee, O Lord, do I lift up	Mr Willm Tucker	83v
Hear my crying, O God (completed at foot of f.83)	Andrew Hecht	83v
'Verse Anthems' (heading)		84
Almighty God, who by the leading of a star	Dr Bull	84
In thee, O Lord, put I my trust	Dr Bull	84
Behold, thou hast made my days	Orlando Gibbons	84-84v
Blessed are all they ('Here is a semibreve rest more yn is in ye Chapel Books')	Orlando Gibbons	84v
The Lord is my light	William Lawes	84v-85
O come hither and hearken	(John Cutts)	85-85v
Lord, how long wilt thou be angry	Willm Tucker	85v
Praise the Lord, ye servants	Willm Tucker	85v
How long wilt thou forget me?	Albertus Bryne	85v-86
Lord, who shall dwell in thy tabernacle?	Mr Portmans	86
I heard a voice from heaven saying, Allelujah	Albertus Bryne	86-86v

Blessed is the man (Ps.1)	Mr Wise	86v-87
Lord, what is man?	Willm Turner	87-87v
Turn thy face from my sins	Matthew Lock	87v
O give thanks (Ps.107)	Wilm Tucker	87v
Wherewithal shall a young man cleanse?	Willm Tucker	88
Behold, how good and joyful a thing	John Blow	88
Awake up my glory	Michael Wise	88
God standeth in the congregation	Henry Hall	88v
I will cry unto thee, O God	John Blow	88v
How are the mighty fallen	Michael Wise	88v
Turn thee unto me	Joh Blow	88v-89
Rejoice in the Lord, O ye righteous	Pelham Humfrey	89
I will magnify thee	Will Tucker	89-89v
I was glad	Will Tucker	89v
By the waters of Babylon	Michael Wise	90
Christ being raised from the dead	John Blow	90-90v
The Lord said unto my Lord	Dr Christopher Gibbons	90v
O Lord, thou hast searched me out	John Blow	90v-91
Rejoice in the Lord, O ye righteous	Richard Portman	91v
Not unto us	Matthew Lock	91v
The earth is the Lord's	Dr Child	92
O be joyful in the Lord	Pelham Humfreys	92-92v
Let God arise	John Ward	92v-93
O Lord, make thy servant Charles	Mr Cranford	93-93v
My song shall be of mercy	Henry Laws	93v
Above the stars the Saviour dwells	Dr Christopher Gibbons	93v-94
How long wilt thou forget me?	Dr Christopher Gibbons	94
My God, my God, look upon me	Thomas Tudway	94-94v

('Organist of King's College in Cambridge')

Save me, O God (Ps.69)	Mr John Blow	105
God be merciful unto us	Dr Christopher Gibbons	105-105v
O Lord, rebuke me not	Dr Childs	105v
Behold, how good and joyful a thing	Dr Childs	106
O Lord my God	Mr Pellham Humfry's	106-106v
Lord, I am not high minded	Dr Christopher Gibbons's	106v
Let God arise	Dr Childs	106v-107
Sing unto the Lord, O ye saints	Dr Christopher Gibbons	107
Out of the deep	Willm Grigory	107-107v
God be merciful unto us	John Blow	107v
Thou art my king, O God	Dr Child	107v
O God, thou hast cast us out	W.Grigoris	108
Awake, awake, put on thy strength	Michael Wise	108v
O praise the Lord, all ye heathen (incomplete)	Henry Pursel	108v
*Prepare ye the way	Mr Wise	109
*O sing unto the Lord (Ps.98)	Dr Child	109
f.109 blank		

Inside back cover: Eight Psalm Tunes (as for Medius Decani)

(5) Medius Cantoris

Inside front cover: Signature 'W.Gostling' and bookplate
Fly-leaf

A Table of all ye Services contained in ys Book   2

f. 2v blank

A Table of all ye Anthems contained in ys Book   3-5

f. 5v blank

Mr Thos Tallis short Service (1,2,4,6,7,8,10)   6-7v

Mr Nicholas Strogers short Service (1,2,4,6,7,8,10)   7v-10

Mr Willm Birds short Service (1,2,4,6,7,8,10)   10-12

Mr Bevins short Service (1,2,4,6,7,8,10)   12-14

Mr Thos Tomkins's short Service (1,2,4,6,7,8,10)   14-16

Mr Orlando Gibbons short Service (1,2,4,6,7,8,10)   16-18

Mr Albertus Brynes short Service (2,5,6,7,8,10)   18-19v

Benjamin Rogers sharp Service (2,5,6,7,8,10)   19v-21

Behold now, praise the Lord   (Dr Rogers)   21-21v
   (at the close of this item:'The end of Mr Rogers
   short sharp service')

Dr Childes sharp Service in D sol re (2,5,6,7,8,10)   21v-23

Dr Childes Service in E minor (2,5,6,7,8,10)   23-25

Dr Child's Service in F (2,5,6,7,9,11)   25-26v

Mr Richard Farrants high Service (2,4,6,7,8,10)   26v-29
   (note: 'This Creed is to be on Decani side
   accordg to Mr Tuckers books')

Mr Portmans Service (2,4,6,7,8,10)   29v-31

Mr Thomas Thomkins Service in D minor (2,5,6,7,8,10)   31-32

Dr Rogers Service in Gamut (2,5,6,7,8,10)   32v-34

Mr Pellam Humfreys short Service in E minor   34-35
   (2,5,6,7,8,10)
   (note at head: 'This part for ye Service is on
   Decani side in Westminster Books'; to 8: 'This
   verse is put on Cantoris side in Westminster
   Books')

Mr John Farrants short Service (2,5,6,7,8,10)   35v-36

Mr Battens short Service (2,5,6,7,8,10)   36-37

Dr Rogers's Service in E la mi (2,5,6,7,8,10)   37-38

Mr Blow's short Service in G (2,5,8,10)   38-38v

Dr Rogers's Service in E la mi (2,5,8,10)   38v-39

Mr Patricks Service (2,4,8,10)   39v-40

Dr Childs Benedicite Service (3,5,6,7,8,10)   40-41

Mr Aldridg's Service in Gamut (2,5,6,7,8,10)   54v-55

Praise the Lord O my soul   Henry Loosmore   55v
  (Ps. 146)

*Blessed is the people   Mr Tudway   55v

*Behold, I bring you glad
  tidings. Xmas Anthem   Henry Purcell   55v-56

A Second Kyrie & Creed in triple time of Dr Blows
  in G   56v

Save me, O God (Ps.54)   Henry Pursel   56v

'Anthems of 5 & 6 Parts & which are for 2 Means'   57
                  (heading)

Save me, O God (Ps.54)   Willm Bird   57

Deliver me from mine enemies   Robert Parsons   57

Sing joyfully   Willm Bird   57v

Hosanna to the Son of David   Orlando Gibbons   57v

Lift up your heads   Orlando Gibbons   58

Lord, who shall dwell in
  thy tabernacle?   (Adrian Batten)   58

O clap your hands   Adrian Batten   58-58v

O give thanks (Ps.105)   Willm Tucker   58v

O come let us sing unto
  the Lord   Robt Ramsey   58v-59

Why art thou so full of
  heaviness?   Thos Wilkinson   59

O Jerusalem, thou that killest
  the prophets   Thos Wilkinson   59-59v

O clap your hands   Willm Tucker   59v

I will sing unto the Lord   Henry Pursell   59v-60

O God, wherefore art thou
  absent?   Mr Blow   60

The king shall rejoice   John Tomkins   60

God is our hope and
  strength (a 8)   John Blow   60v

O clap your hands (Dr Hethers
  Commencement Song')   Orlando Gibbons   60v-61

Inclina Domine   (Mr Ramsy)   61-61v

O praise God in his holiness   Willm White   61v

*Mr Purcells Service in B flat (2,4,6,7,8,10)   61v-62

    The number 63, by accident, has not been used in foliation.

  f. 64 blank

Holy, holy, holy	Adrian Batten	64v
Unto thee, O Lord	Richard Dering	64v
Let God arise	Dr Child	64v
'Verse Anthems' (heading)		65
Almighty God, who by the leading of a star	Dr Bull	65
Blessed are all they	(Orlando Gibbons)	65-65v
My heart is fixed	Willm Tucker	65v-66
Sing we merrily	John Blow	66
I will alway give thanks	Pelham Humfreys, John Blow, and William Turner	66
I am well pleased	Willm Tucker	66v
Above the stars the Saviour dwells	Dr Christopher Gibbons	67
Behold I bring you glad tidings	Benjamin Rogers	67-67v
How long wilt thou forget me?	Albertus Bryne	67v
My beloved spake (with an amendment: 'Thus in ye printed books')	Thomas Tomkins	67v-68
O how amiable are thy dwellings	Mr Loe (?Edward Lowe)	68
How long wilt thou forget me? (with an amendment: 'Thus in Westminster Books')	Dr Christopher Gibbons	68v
Above the stars the Saviour dwells	Dr Christopher Gibbons	68v-69
Unto thee I Lord do I lift up	Willm Tucker	69-69v
Lord who shall dwell in thy tabernacle?	Mr Portmans	69v
O Lord, thou hast searched me out	Adrian Batten	69v-70
I heard a voice in heaven saying, Allelujah	Albertus Bryne	70-70v
Blessed is the man (Ps.1)	Michael Wise	70v
Lord, what is man?	Willm Turner	70v
Lord, let me know mine end	(Matthew Lock)	70v-71

Awake my soul, that too securely sleep'st	Mr George Jefferys	78v
Help me, Lord	Dr Christopher Gibbons	79
Turn thou us, O good Lord	George Jefferys	79-79v
Great and marvellous are thy works	George Jefferys	79v
Turn thee again, O Lord God of hosts	George Jeffrys	80
How wretched is the state	George Jeffrys	80-80v
O Domine Deus, O amabile	George Jeffrys	80v
O Deus meus	George Jeffrys	80v-81
Lord, come away	Isaac Blackwell	81
Have pity upon me, O ye friends	Dr Christopher Gibbons	81-81v
O God, thou art my God	Isaack Blackwell	81v-82
God is our hope and strength	Silas Taylor	82-82v
Bow down thine ear	Isaack Blackwell	82v
Sing unto the Lord, O ye saints	Dr Christopher Gibbons	83
Out of the deep	Will Grigory	83
God be merciful unto us	John Blow	83v
Give the king thy judgments	Mr Henry Alldridge	83v
Give sentence with me	Henry Pursell	83v
*O give thanks. . . and his mercy	(Dr Aldridge)	84
*Behold now, praise the Lord	Dr Blow	84
*Have pity upon me, O ye friends (concluded at foot of f.83v)	Mr Wise	84
*Hear my prayer, O Lord (Ps.102)	Mr Turners	84v
*My God, my God, look upon me	Dr Blow	84v
*I waited patiently	Dr Blow	85-85v
*Try me, O God	Dr Turner	85v
*O God, thou art my God	Mr Purcell	85v-86
*O sing unto God	Dr Blow	86

*O God, thou hast cast us out	Mr Purcell	87
*Thy word is a lantern (incomplete)	(Mr Purcell)	87
*O be joyful in God	Dr Blow	87
*God is our hope and strength (contratenor)	(Dr Aldrich)	87v
*God is our hope and strength (medius) (concluded at foot of f.87)	(Dr Aldrich)	87v

(6) Contratenor Cantoris

Mr Aldridg's Evening Service in G (8,10)		59v
The 2d Creed to Dr Blows Service in G (triple time)		59v-60
*Mr Purcells Service in B flat (2,4,6,7,8,10)		60-60v
ff.61-64v blank		
*O sing unto God	John Blow	65-65v
*O Lord God, to whom vengeance belongeth	J sine nomine B (recte: John Blow?)	65v
*Rogers in A (8,10)		
*My God, my God, look upon me	Dr Blow	66v
*Try me, O God	(Dr Turner)	66v
*I will sing a new song	Mr Wise	67
O Lord, I have loved the habitation	Tho Tomkins	67v
Save me, O God (Ps.54)	Henry Pursel	67v
'Full Anthems of 5 Parts' (heading)		68
With all our hearts	Thos Tallis	68
Blessed be thy name	Tho Tallis	68
O thou God, Almighty Father	Edmund Hooper	68
O Lord, I bow the knees	Willm Mundy	68-68v
I call and cry	(Thomas Tallis)	68v
Prevent us, O Lord (composer's name cropped in binding)	William Byrd	68v-69
Behold, it is Christ	Edm Hooper	69
O Lord, make thy servant Charles	Willm Bird	69
I lift my heart to thee	Dr Tye	69-69v
O Lord, turn thy wrath (with 2nd part,'Bow thine ear')	Willm Bird	69v-70
O give thanks	Dr Giles	70
Almighty God, the fountain of all wisdom	Tho Tomkins	70-70v
Why art thou so full of heaviness?	Thos Wilkinson	70v
O Jerusalem, thou that killest the prophets	Thos Wilkinson	70v-71
We beseech thee, Almighty God	Adrian Batten	71
Lord, who shall dwell in thy tabernacle?	Adrian Batten	71

'The Second Contratenor of ye vers Anthems' (heading) 80

Behold thou hast made my days	Orlando Gibbons	80
Blessed are all they	Orlando Gibbons	80
Behold, I bring you glad tidings	Orlando Gibbons	80-80v
How long wilt thou forget me?	Thos Morley	80v-81
Almighty God, who by the leading of a star (note: part of the composer's name cropped in binding)	Dr Bull	81
In thee, O Lord, put I my trust	Dr Bull	81-81v
O Lord, let me know mine end	Tho Tomkins	81v
Let God arise	John Ward	81v
Hear my prayer O Lord, hold not thy peace	Thos Wilkinson	81v-82
Thou art my King, O God	Tho Tomkins	82
Out of the deep	Thos Morley	82
I heard a voice in heaven saying, Allelujah	Albert Bryne	82-82v
O praise God in his holiness	Edm Smith (recte Edward)	82v
O how happy a thing it is	Adrian Batten	82v
The earth is the Lords	Willm Turner	83
O be joyful in God	Willm Turner	83-83v
Blessed is the man (Psalm 1)	Andreas Hecht	83v-84
Lord, who shall dwell in thy tabernacle?	Andreas Hecht	84
O come hither and hearken	(John Cutts)	84v
Lord, how long wilt thou be angry?	Wm Tucker	84v-85
Praise the Lord, ye servants	W. Tucker	85-85v
Lord, who shall dwell in thy tabernacle?	Mr Portman	85v-86
O Lord, thou hast searched me out	Adrian Batten	86
How long wilt thou forget me?	Albert Bryne	86-86v

I heard a voice from heaven saying, Allelujah	Albert Bryne	86v-87
Belssed is the man (Psalm 1)	Michael Wise	87
Lord, what is man?	Will Turner	87-87v
Lord, let me know mine end	Matthew Lock	87v-88
Turn thy face from my sins	Matthew Lock	88
Behold now, praise the Lord	John Blow	88
'Verse Anthems' (heading)		88v
The Lord said unto my Lord ('The 3d Treble')	Dr Christopher Gibbons	88v
Rejoice in the Lord, O ye righteous	Richard Portman	88v
Not unto us	Matthew Lock	88v-89
O be joyful in the Lord	Pelham Humfrys	89
The earth is the Lords	Dr Child	89v
This is the day (note: 'ys Anthem is on Decany side')	Willm Tucker	89v-90
Comfort ye, my people	Willm Tucker	89v-90
O Lord our governor	Henry Pursell	90v
I wil alway give thanks	Pellham Humfrys John Blow, Willm Turner	90v-91
By the waters of Babylon	Henry Hall	91-91v
I will praise the Lord	John Ward	91v
Holy, holy, holy	Adrian Batten	91v-92
Unto thee, O Lord	Richard Deering	92
O give thanks (Ps.118)	Pellam Humfrys	92-92v
O Lord, rebuke me not	Dr Child	92v-93
Behold, how good and joyful a thing	Dr Child	93
O Lord, my God	P.Humfrys	93-93v
Awake, my soul	George Jeffrys	93v
Help me, Lord	Dr Christopher Gibbons	93v
Turn thou us, O good Lord	George Jeffrys	93v-94
Great and marvellous	George Jeffrys	94-94v
Turn thee again	George Jeffrys	94v
How wretched is the state	George Jeffrys	94v-95
Domine Deo, O amabile principia	George Jeffrys	95
O Deus meus	George Jeffrys	95-95v

O Lord, come away	Isaac Blackwell	95v
Have pity on me, O ye friends	Dr Christopher Gibbons	95v-96
O God, thou art my God	Isaac Blackwell	96
God is our hope and strength	Silas Taylor	96-96v
Bow down thine ear	Isaac Blackwell	96v-97
Let God arise	Dr Child	97
Give the King thy judgments	Mr Henry Alldridge	97
Give sentence with me (note: composer's name added by Gostling)	H.Pursel	97-97v
*Blessed is the people	Mr Tudway	97v
*Behold now, praise the Lord	John Blow	97v
*I was glad	(Mr Purcel)	97v-98
*I beheld, and lo! a great multitude	Dr Rogers	98
*O God. thou hast cast us out	Mr Purcell	98v
*Hide not thou thy face	(Aldrich upon Farrant)	99
*Give sentence with me	(Dr Aldrich) based on O.Gibbons,'Almighty and everlasting God'	99

(7) Tenor Cantoris

Inside front cover: 'W.Gosling' and bookplate (bookplate also inside back cover)
Recipe or prescription in John Gostling's hand: 1
  ½ pint of sack
    of oil of sweet Almons
  Ditto oil of Rhow (? rhodium)
  for a Clyster probatium (last three letters doubtful)
f.1v blank

A Table of all ye Services contained in ys Book   2

f.2v blank

A Table of all ye Anthems contained in ys Book   3-5

f.5v blank

Mr Thos Tallis short Service (1,2,4,6,7,8)   6-7v
                    (incomplete)

Mr Strogers short Service (1,2,4,6,7,8,10)   8-10

Mr Birds short Service (1,2,4,6,7,8,10)   10-12

Mr Thos Tomkins short Service (1,2,4,6,7,8,10)   12v-14v
  (note in (8) with amendment:'so in Westminster
  books')

Mr Bevins short Service   14v-16v

Mr Orlando Gibbons short Service (1,2,4,6,7,8,10)   16v-18

Mr Albertus Brynes short Service (2,5,6,7,8,10)   18v-19v

Mr Ben Rogers short sharp Service (2,5,6,7,8,10)   20-21

Behold now, praise the Lord   (Dr Rogers)   21-21v

Dr Childes sharp Service in D sol re (2,5,8,10)   21v-23

The Keery & Creed of Dr Childs sharp Service in D   23-23v
  (6,7)

Dr Childes Service in E minor (2,5,6,7,8,10)   23v-24v

Dr Childes Service in F (2,5,6,7,9,11)   24v-26

Mr Richard Farrants high Service (2,4,6,7,8,10)   26-28

Mr Portmans Service (2,4,6,7,8,10)   28-29v

Mr Thomas Tomkins's Service in D minor   29v-31v
  (2,5,6,7,8,10)

Dr Rogers's Service in Gamut (2,5,6,7,8,10)   31v-32v

Mr Pelham Humfreys Short Service in E la mi   33-33v
  (2,5,6,7,8,10)

Mr John Farrants short Service (2,5,6,7,8,10)   33v-34v
  (note: 'This Service in on Decani side see p.72
  (f.41v) for yt on Cantoris side')

Mr Battens short Service (2,5,6,7,8,10)   34v-35v

78

*Thy way, O God	Mr Purcell	56
Dr Heathers Commencement Song composed by Mr Orlando Gibbons O clap your hands		56v
'Anthems of 4. voyces' (heading)		57
O God, whose never failing providence	Andreas Hecht	57
When the Lord turned again	Adrian Batten	57
Call to remembrance	Richard Farrant	57-57v
Hide not thou thy face	Richard Farrant	57v
Let my complaint	Adrian Batten	57v
God is our hope (a 8)	Mr Blow	57v
'Full Anthems of 5 Parts & allso of 6 parts' (heading)		58
O come, let us sing unto the Lord	Robert Ramsey	58
Hosanna to the Son of David	Orlando Gibbons	58
*When the Son of Man shall come	Dr Blow	58
O clap your hands	Adrian Batten	58v
Why art thou so full of heaviness?	Thos Wilkinson	58v
O Jerusalem, thou that killest	Thos Wilkinson	58v-59
Turn thy face from my sins	Matthew Lock	59-59v
I will sing unto the Lord	Henry Pursel	59v
O clap your hands together	Willm Tucker	59v-60
O God, wherefore art thou absent?	Mr Blow	60
O Lord, I have loved the habitation	Thomas Tomkins	60
'Vers Anthems' (heading)		60v
Sing unto the Lord, O ye kingdoms	Will Turner	60v
This is the day	Willm Turner	60v-61
Praise the Lord, O my soul (Ps. 103)	(Mr Hecht)	61-61v
My days are gone	John Cutts	61v
O praise the Lord, ye angels	John Cutts	61v-62
O sing unto the Lord (Psalm 98)	John Cutts	62
O sing unto the Lord for it is a good thing	Willm Turner	62-62v
Hear my crying, O God	Andreas Hecht	62v-64

By the waters of Babylon	John Cuts	64-64v
Praise the Lord, ye servants (ending on a slip, f.65)	Andreas Hecht	64v
Lord who shall dwell in thy tabernacle? (composer's name cropped in binding)	Andreas Hecht	64v-66
Haste thee, O God	Andreas Hecht	66
The earth is the Lord's	Willm Turner	66v
O Lord, thou hast searched me out	Adrian Batten	66v
Lord, how long wilt thou forget me?	Albertus Bryne	67
I heard a voice from heaven saying, Allelujah	Albertus Bryne	67
Blessed is the man(Psalm 1)	Mr Wise	67
Lord, what is man?	Willm Turner	67v
Lord let me know mine end	Matthew Lock	68
Turn thy face from my sins	Matthew Lock	67v
Lord, how are they increased	John Blow	68-68v
I will cry unto thee, O God	John Blow	69
Rejoice in the Lord, O ye righteous	Pelham Humfrey	69
Rejoice in the Lord, O ye righteous	Richard Portman	69
Not unto us	Matthew Lock	69v
The earth is the Lord's	Dr Child	69v
O be joyful in the Lord	Pelham Humfreys	69v
Blessed are all they that fear the Lord	Orlando Gibbons	70
Almighty God, who by the leading of a star	Dr Bull	70
Haste thee, O God	Pellham Humfrys	70v
I am well pleased	Will Tucker	70v
My heart is fixed	Will Tucker	71
By the waters of Babylon	Mr Henry Hall	71v-72
Behold, God is my salvation	Mr Tudway	72-72v
O give thanks (Psalm 118)	Mr Pellham Humfrys	72v

Not unto us (note:'as it is in Mr Tuckers book')	Matthew Lock	73
Blow up the trumpet	Mr Henry Pursel	73
Blow up the trumpet (contra tenor) (note: 'The Contratenor & Tenor for ys Anthem are here to sing together')	Henry Pursel	73
O Lord, rebuke me not	Dr Childs	73v
Behold, how good and jouful a thing	Dr Childs	73v
O Lord my God	Mr Pellham Humfrys	74
Awake my soul, thou too securely sleep'st	George Jeffrys	74
Help me, Lord	Dr Christopher Gibbons	74
Turn thou us, O good Lord	George Jeffrys	74v
Great and marvellous are thy works	George Jeffrys	75
Turn thee again, O Lord God	George Jeffrys	75-75v
How wretched is the state	George Jeffrys	75v-76
O Domine Deus	George Jeffrys	76
O Deus meus	George Jeffrys	76-76v
Lord, come away	Isaack Blackwell	76v
Have pity upon me, O ye friends	Dr Christopher Gibbons	76v-77
O God, thou art my God	Isaack Blackwell	77-77v
God is our hope and strength	Silas Taylor	77v
Bow down thine ear	Isaack Blackwell	77v-78
Let God arise	Dr Child	78
O praise the Lord all ye heathen	Henry Pursell	78v
Give the King thy judgments	Mr Henry Alldridge	78v
Give sentence with me	Henry Pursell	78v-79
*O sing unto the Lord (Psalm 98)	(Dr Child)	79
*O give thanks ...and his mercy	Dr Aldridge	79v
*Lord, teach us to number our days	Mr Humphreys	79v-80
*Behold now praise the Lord	Dr Blow	80
*Have pity upon me, O ye my friends	Mr Wise	80

*Hear my prayer, O Lord (Ps. 102)	Mr Turner	80v
*I was glad	(Mr Purcel)	81
*Hear, O heavens	Pelham Humfrey	81v
*I will alway give thanks	Pelham Humfrey, John Blow, William Turner	81v-82
*I beheld, and lo! a great multitude	Dr Rogers	82-82v
*I will sing a new song	(Mr Wise)	82v
*Prepare ye the way	Mr Wise	83
*O praise God in his holiness	Mr Wise	83v
*O clap your hands	Dr Rogers	83v
*O clap your hands (Medius part)	Benjamin Rogers	84
*The Lord said unto my Lord (also Medius part)	Mr Wise	84-84v
*O give thanks (Psalm 106)	Mr Pursell	84v-85
*Teach me, O Lord (Medius part)	Christopher Gibbons	85v
*Teach me, O Lord	Dr Christopher Gibbons	86
*O God, thou art my God	Mr Purcell	86
*Behold, I bring you glad tidings	Mr Purcell	86v-87
*Out of the deep	Dr Aldrich	87
*O praise the Lord, laud ye the name	Dr Child	87v
*I waited patiently	Dr Blow	87v
*Try me, O God	Dr Turner	88
*O God, thou art my God (Decani part)	Mr Purcell	88-88v
*O God, thou art my God (Cantoris part)	Mr Purcell	88v
*O God, thou hast cast us out (Cantoris with Decani part)	Mr Purcell	89
*O sing unto God	Dr Blow	89-89v
*Sing we merrily	Dr Blow	89v-90
*O Lord God, to whom vengeance belongeth	J sine nomine B (recte John Blow?)	90
*God is our hope and strength	(Dr Aldrich)	90v

(8) Bassus Cantoris

Inside front cover: Signature 'W.Gostling' and bookplate
Memorandum:
  Munday being 28 April 79 about 1 of ye clock in ye daytime
  was Mr Airsdens will was open'd in ye presence of ye
  Principle of Clifforss Inn & me Stephen Bing
Inside back cover: crude note, 'Mr John A. E. (?N)'

Tuckers Evening to his Benedicite Service (8,10)   39

His (i.e., William Tucker's) short Service   39-39v
    (2,5,8,10)

Mr John Amners Caesars Service (2,5,6,7,8,10)   40-41

O come hither and hearken   John Amner
                                   Organist of Ely   41

Mr Patricks Kyriee & Creed   41-41v

Mr Blows Service in A re (2,5,6,7,9,11)   41v-42

Mr Wise's Morning & Evening Service for Verses
    in D minor (2,5,8,10)   42v

Dr Childs Service in A re (i.e., A minor)   43-43v
    (2,5,6,7,8,10)

Dr Childs Service in E flatt (2,5,6,7,8,10)   43v-44

Dr Childs Te Deum in Gamut or Benedicite Service   44-44v

Dr Childs Evening Service in G (9,11)   44v

Dr Childs Creed to his Service in E flatt   45
    (7, also 8,10)

Dr Childs Te Deum to his Benedicite Service   45-45v

Mr Blows Benedicite or his Service in E la mi   45v-46v
    (3,5,6,7,9,11)

Mr Blows Kyrie & Creed in Gamut   46v

Mr Wises Commandments & Creed to his Service
    in D sol re   46v-47

Dr Blow's Te Deum to his benedicite Service   47

Mr Henry Alldridg's Service in E la mi(3,5,6,7,8,10)   47-48

Mr John Ferabosco's Evening Service (8,10)   48

Mr Aldridgs Service in Gamut (2,5,6,7,8,10)   48-48v

Anthems of 5 voyces (heading)   49

O come, let us sing unto the
    Lord   Robert Ramsy   49

Why art thou so full of
    heaviness?   Thomas Wilkinson   49

O Jerusalem, thou that killest
    the prophets   Mr Wilkinson   49-49v

Turn thy face from my sins   Matthew Locke   49v

I will sing unto the Lord   Henry Pursel   50

O clap your hands together   Willm Tucker   50

Save me, O God (Ps. 54)   Henry Pursel   50v

Dr Blows Second Creed in G (triple time) (also 6)   50v

*The King shall rejoice   John Tomkins   50v-51

Holy, holy, holy	Adrian Batten	71v
Not unto us	Matthew Lock	71v
*O give thanks ... and his mercy	Mr Aldridge	71v
How long wilt thou forget me?	Albertus Bryne	72
I heard a voice from heaven saying, Allelujah	Albertus Bryne	72-72v
"Vers Anthems' (heading)		
Blessed is the man (Ps.1)	Mr Wise	72v-73
Lord, what is man?	Willm Turner	73
Lord, let me know mine end	Matthew Locke	73-73v
Turn thy face from my sins	Matthew Lock	73v
O Lord, thou hast searched me out	John Blow	73v-74
Rejoice in the Lord, O ye righteous	Richard Portman	74
Not unto us	Matthew Lock	74v
The earth is the Lord's	Dr Child	74v
O be joyful in the Lord	Pelham Humfrys	75
Let God arise	John Ward	75-75v
O Lord our governor	Henry Pursell	75v-76
My heart is fixed	Wilm Tucker	76
I will alway give thanks	Pellham Humfrys, John Blow, W.Turner	76-76v
Haste thee, O God	Pellham Humfrys	76v
Sing we merrily	John Blow	76v
I am well pleased	W.Tucker	76v
By the waters of Babylon	Henry Hall	77
Blow up the trumpet	Henry Purcell	77v
Behold, God is my salvation	Thomas Tudway	77v
O God, wherefore art thou absent?	Mr Blow	77v-78
Awake, my soul, that too securely sleep'st	George Jeffrys	78
Help me, Lord	Dr Christopher Gibbons	78-78v
Turn thou us, O good Lord	George Jeffrys	78v
Great and marvellous	George Jeffrys	78v179

Turn thee again, O Lord God of hosts	George Jeffrys	79-79v
How wretched is the state	George Jeffrys	79v
O Domine Deus	George Jeffrys	79v-80
O Deus meus	George Jeffrys	80
Lord, come away	Isaack Blackwell	80v
Have pity upon me, O ye friends	Dr Christopher Gibbons	80v
O God, thou art my God	Isaac Blackwell	80v-81
God is our hope and strength	Silas Taylor	81-81v
Bow down thine ear, O Lord	Isaac Blackwell	81v-82
Let God arise	Dr Childs	82
Give the King thy judgments	Mr Aldridge	82-82v
Give sentence with me	Henry Pursell	82v
*Praise the Lord, O my soul, while I live	Henry Loosmore	83
*Have pity upon me, O ye my friends	Mr Wise	83v
*Hear my prayer, O Lord (Ps. 102)	Mr Turner	83v
*Sing unto the Lord, O ye kingdoms	Mr Turner	84
f.84v blank		

Index to Catalogue

M – Medius; C-t – Contratenor; T – Tenor; B – Bassus

	Decani				Cantoris			
	M	C-t	T	B	M	C-t	T	B
Anonymous								
Look, shepherds, look			72v					
Aldrich (Henry) 1648–1710								
'Benedicite' Service in E minor	58	46v	103v	45	52v 54	56	49v	47
Service in G	58v	47v	104v	45v	54v	57v 59	51v	48
Give sentence with me (based on O Gibbons, 'Almighty and everlasting God')	114v					99	91	63v
Give the king thy judgments					83v	97	78v	82
God is our hope and strength	114				87v		90v	63
O give thanks ...and his mercy	71	57			84	77v 78	79v	71v
Out of the deep	38v	61		58v			87	
See also R.Farrant								
Amner (John) 1579–1641								
'Caesar's' Service in G	46v	38v	40v	35	43v	46	43	40
Short, or Third Service	48v		42v	36v		48		
O come hither, and hearken	48	40	42v	36v	45	47v	44v	41
Batten (Adrian) 1591–1637								
Short Service	34v	31v	35	30	36	38 50v	34v 42	33
Christ rising again		84v	84					
Deliver us, O Lord	45	54v	54	53v				
Haste thee, O God (with 2nd part, But let all those that seek thee)	41v	53v	52v	52v				

	Decani				Cantoris			
	M	C-t	T	B	M	C-t	T	B
Hear my prayer, O God	101v	70v	60	67		71v		
Hide not thou thy face	41	53	52	67v				
Holy, holy, holy	87	77v	68v	52	64v	91v		71v
Let my complaint come before thee	62	56v	56v	81	53v	59	57v	52v
Lord, we beseech thee give ear	41v	53	52v	54v				
Lord, who shall dwell in thy tabernacle?	76	70v	63	52v	58	71		
My soul truly waiteth	45	54v	54	77				
O clap your hands	76	71	63v	53v				
O how happy a thing it is	94v	84	82	76v	58	77v	58v	68
O Lord our governor	95	85	79	99v		82v		
O Lord, thou hast searched me out	101v			77	69v	86	66v	
O praise the Lord, all ye heathen	40v	53	52	52				
O sing joyfully	45v	55	54v	53v				
Out of the deep (Daniel & Le Huray, Version I)	88v	91v	78	80v				
We beseech thee, Almighty God	69	70v	60v	67		71		
When the Lord turned again the captivity	41v	53v	52v	52v	53	58v	57	52

Bevin (Elway) c1554-1638

	Decani				Cantoris			
	M	C-t	T	B	M	C-t	T	B
Short, or First Service	11v	12	14	11	12	14	14v	12

Blackwell (Isaac) fl1674-87

	Decani				Cantoris			
	M	C-t	T	B	M	C-t	T	B
Bow down thine ear					82v	96v	77v	81v
Lord, come away					81	95v	76v	80v
O God, thou art my God					81v	96	77	80v

	Decani				Cantoris			
	M	C-t	T	B	M	C-t	T	B
Blow (John) 1649-1708								
Service in A	50v	40v	44v	38v	45v	51v	45	41v
'Benedicite' Service in E minor	54v	37	48	42	50	44v	40v	45v 47v
Te Deum to Service in E minor	57 63	46v	103	44v 48	52	56	49	47 54
Morning and Evening Service in G	36v	33v	37	31v	38	40	36v	35
Communion Service in G	56v	44v	47v	43v	51	55v	48v	46v
Second Communion Service in G, triple time	59v	48v	49v	46v	56v	59v	51	50v
Behold, how good and joyful a thing	104v	94v	88	88				
Behold now, praise the Lord	81		88		84	88 97v	80	
Christ being raised from the dead	106v 107 110v 112v	97 102v 107v	90v 95v 101	90 99 107v	83v			
God be merciful unto us	76v	76v	68v	75v	60v	75v	57v	68
God is our hope and strength (a 8)	73	62		71	85		87v	
I waited patiently			88v	88v			69	
I will cry unto thee, O God	105	95	87v	95			68	
Lord, how are they increased	104	94v						
My God, my God, look upon me				71v	84v 87	66v	55v	69v
O be joyful in God		62v						
O God, wherefore art thou absent?	70	76v	100	104v	60	73	60	77v
O how amiable are thy dwellings	79v	104v	98v	102				
O Lord God to whom vengeance belongeth	113v			59		65v	90	
O Lord, I have sinned	110	102	95v	98v				
O Lord, thou hast searched me out	80 86v	97v	91v	90v				73v
O sing unto God					86	65	89v	62v

	Decani				Cantoris			
	M	C-t	T	B	M	C-t	T	B
Save me, O God (Ps.69)	70v	77	61v	105		76		
Sing we merrily	86v	100v	94	97	66		89v	76v
The Lord hear thee	62v	57	56	55v				
Turn thee unto me	105v	95v 99v	89v	88v				
When the Son of Man shall come	113v			71		78	58	
Bryne/Bryan (Albertus) c1621-1671								
Short Service in G	15v	15v	17	14v	18	18	18v	16
How long wilt thou forget me?	92	83v	80v	85v	67v	86	67	72
I heard a voice in heaven saying, Allelujah	102	82v	73	86	70	82 86v	67	72
Bull (John) ?1562 or 3 - 1628								
Almighty God, which by the leading of a star	90	79	74v 108v	84	65 74v	81	70	
In thee, O Lord, put I my trust	90	79	69	84		81		
Byrd/Bird (William) 1543 - 1623								
Short Service	8	8v	10v	7v	10	9v	10	8
O Lord, make thy servant Charles	66	68	58	65		69		
O Lord, turn thy wrath (with 2nd part, Bow thine ear)	66v	68v	58v	65v		69v		
Prevent us, O Lord	65v	67v	57v	64v		68v		
Save me, O God (Ps.54)	68v	70	69 82v	67	57			
Sing joyfully	75	75v	63	76	57v	76v		

Child (William) 1606 or 7 – 1697

	Decani				Cantoris			
	M	C-t	T	B	M	C-t	T	B
Service in A minor	52	42	46	40	47v	53v	46v	43
Service in D	18v	17v	19v	17	21v	21	21v	19
Service in E minor	20v	19v, 45	21	18v	23	23	23v	21v
'Flat' Service in E	53	43	107v	40v	48v	54	47	43v, 45
Service in F	23	20v	22	19v	25	25	24v	22v
'Benedicite' Service in G	38	35	38v	33	40	41v	38	36v
Service in G, alternative Canticles	54	43v	47	41v	47v, 49	53, 55	46v, 48	44, 45
Behold, how good and joyful a thing	111	107v	100v	106	78	93	73v	
If the Lord himself	46	55v	55	54v				
Let God arise	111v	107	100v	106v	64v	97	78	82
O clap your hands	45v	55v	54v	54v				
O Lord, grant the king a long life	45v	55v	55	54				
O Lord, rebuke me not (Daniels & le Huray, Version I)	72v, 74v		100v	105v	78	92v	73v	
O praise the Lord (Ps. 135)		61v		58v			87v	
O pray for the peace of Jerusalem	46	56	54v	55	53, 78	58		
O sing unto the Lord (Ps. 98)	75, 78	108v		109			79	
Praise the Lord, O my soul (Ps.103)	45	55	55v	54				
The earth is the Lord's		99v	92	92	74	89v	69v	74v
Thou art my king, O God	112v	107v	101	107v				

	Decani				Cantoris			
	M	C-t	T	B	M	C-t	T	B
Cranford (William) c1650-1675								
O Lord, make thy servant Charles	93v	82	76	93				
Cutts (John) *1691 or 2								
By the waters of Babylon	83	86	71v				64	
I give you a new commandment (Ps.138)	42v	54v	53	53				
I will give thanks	100	92	84v					
I will magnify thee	94v	85	77					
Let thy merciful ears			54					
My days are gone	84v	87v	71				61v	
O come hither and hearken	100v	87v	85			84v		38v
O praise the Lord, ye angels	85	88	71	85			61v	
O sing unto the Lord (Ps. 98)	85v	88	71				62	
Dering (Richard) c1580 - 1630								
Unto thee, O Lord, will I lift up	87	77v	68v	81	64v	92		
Farrant (John) fl pre-Civil War								
Short Service	33v	31	34v	29v	35v	37 / 49v	33v / 41v	32
Farrant (Richard) *1581								
'High' Service in A minor	24	22	23v	21	26v	26v	26	24
Call to remembrance	39	51v	50v	50v	53v	58v	57	52
Hide not thy face	39v	51v	50v	50v	53v	58v	57v	52v
-ditto- adapted by Aldrich	114					99	91	63v

Ferrabosco (John) 1626-1682

Gibbons (Christopher) 1615-1676

Gibbons (Orlando) 1583 - 1625

	Decani				Cantoris			
	M	C-t	T	B	M	C-t	T	B
Verse Evening Service	57v	47v	104	45v	52v	57	50	48
Above the stars the Saviour dwells	95v	85v	70v	93v	67, 68v, 76v			
God be merciful unto us	110v	105	100	105	81	95v	76v	80v
Have pity upon me, O ye friends					79	93v	74	78
Help me, Lord					68v			
How long wilt thou forget me?	92v	85v	83	94	68v			
Lord, I am not highminded	111v	78v	68	106v	78v			
O praise the Lord, all ye heathen	108	101v	95	98	73v			
Sing unto the Lord, O ye saints	112	107		107	83			
Teach me, O Lord	82v	60		78			85v, 86	
The Lord said unto my Lord	107v	101v	91	90v	73v	88v		
Short Service	14	13v	15v	13v	16	16	16v	14
Almighty and everlasting God	40v	52v	51v	51v				
Behold, I bring you glad tidings	91	79v	73	81v		80		
Behold, thou hast made my days	90v	79v	75	84		80		
Blessed are all they	90v	79v	75v	84v	65, 74v	80	70	
Deliver us, O Lord (with 2nd part, Blessed be the Lord God)	41	53	52	52				

	Decani				Cantoris			
	M	C-t	T	B	M	C-t	T	B
Glorious and powerful God	91	80	78v	81v				
Hosanna to the Son of David	75v	76	63v	76	57v	77	58	
If ye be risen again with Christ	91v	80v	83	81v	76v	77		
Lift up your heads	75v	76	64	76v	58	77		
O clap your hands (with 2nd part 'God is gone up')	76v	75	64v	75	60v	75	56v	68v
See also Aldrich								
Giles (Nathaniel) c1558 - 1634								
O give thanks (eclectic text)	67	69	59	65v		70		
Gregory (William fl 1651 - 1687								
O God, thou hast cast us out	113	107v	101	108				
Out of the deep	112	107	101	107	83			
Hall Henry c1656 - 1707								
By the waters of Babylon		102v	88v	88v	76	91	71v	77
God standeth in the congregation	104v	95	88v	88v	72			
Heardson (Thomas)								
Almighty God, we beseech thee, give ear	38v	51	50	50				
Keep, we beseech thee, O good Lord	39	51v	50v	50v				
Hecht (Andreas)								
Blessed is the man (Ps.1)	84	86v	74			83v		
Haste thee, O God	85	90	72	82v			66	
Hear my crying, O God	83 98v	90v	71v	83v			62v	

	Decani				Cantoris			
	M	C-t	T	B	M	C-t	T	B
Lord, who shall dwell in thy tabernacle?	84v	92	72			84	64v	
O God, whose neverfailing providence	42	53v	53	53	53	58	57	52
Praise the Lord, O my soul (Ps.103)	84v		69 70v				61	
Praise the Lord, ye servants	83	78v	71v	83			64v	
Henstridge (Daniel) c1646 – 1737								
Verse Service	59v							
Hooper (Edmund) c1553 – 1621								
Behold, it is Christ	66	68	58	65		69		
O thou God, Almighty Father	65	67	57	64		68		
Teach me thy way	40v	52v	51v	51v				
Humfrey (Pelham) 1647 – 1674								
Short Service in E minor	32v	30	33v	29	34	36	33	31v
By the waters of Babylon	87v	103	96v	99v				
Haste thee, O God		99	93 94v	95	75v		70v	76v
Have mercy upon me (Musica Britannica, vol. 34, version II)	110	101v	95	98				
Hear, O heavens	79v	105v	98	102			81v	
Like as the hart	80v	105	99v	104			79v	
Lord, teach us to number our days	80	106	99	103				
O be joyful in the Lord		99	99v	92	74v	89	69v	75
O give thanks (Ps. 118)	80	106	105	103v		92	72v	

	Decani				Cantoris			
	M	C-t	T	B	M	C-t	T	B
O Lord, my God		106v	100v	106	77v	93	74	
Rejoice in the Lord, O ye righteous	106	95v	89v	89	66	90v	69	
(with John Blow and William Turner: I will alway give thanks)	81v	101	94v	97			81v	76
Jeffreys (George) c1610 - 1685								
Awake, my soul, that too securely sleep'st					78v	93v	74	78
Great and marvellous are thy works					79v	94	75	78v
How wretched is the state					80	94v	75v	79v
O Domine Deus (with 2nd part, O Deus meus)					80v	95	76	79v
Turn thee again, O Lord God of hosts					80	94v	75	79
Turn thou us, O good Lord					79	93v	74v	78v
King (William) 1624 - 1680								
Now that the Lord hath re-advanced the crown	93v	83	78					
O sing unto the Lord (Ps. 149)		84v	84v					
Lawes (Henry) 1596 - 1662								
My song shall be of mercy	93v	83	77v	93v				
Zadok the priest	42	54	83	53				
Lawes (William) 1602 - 1645								
Let God arise	87v	103v	97	100v				
The Lord is my light	98	92v	85	84v				
Locke (Matthew) 1621 or 2 - 1677								
Lord, let me know mine end	102v	93v	86v	77v	70v	87v	68	73

	Decani				Cantoris			
	M	C-t	T	B	M	C-t	T	B
Not unto us (Musica Britannica, vol. 38, "A")	108v	98	91v	91v	74	88v	69v	74v
Not unto us (Musica Britannica, vol. 38, "B")	87v	103	97	100	77	79v	73	71v
Turn thy face from my sins	103	71v	87	87v	71	88	59 / 67v	49v / 73v
Loosemore (George) *1682								
O that mine eyes would melt	96v		73v					
Loosemore (Henry) *1670								
Let all the world in every corner sing	94	83v	82					83
Praise the Lord, O my soul (Ps.146)		73v	68		55v			
Lowe (Edward) c1610 - 1682								
O how amiable are thy dwellings	94		80v	80v	68			
Morley (Thomas) 1557 or 8 - 1602								
How long wilt thou forget me?	92	81	83v			80v		
Out of the deep	91v	80v	74v	80v		82		
Mundy (William) c1529 - ?1591								
Service in D minor	28v	26v	29	25v		32		
O Lord, I bow the knees of my heart	65	67	57	64v		68		
O Lord, the maker of all thing	40	52	51	51				
O Lord, the world's Saviour	40	52v	51v	51v				
Parsons (Robert) c1530 - 1570								
Deliver me from mine enemies	75	75v	63	76	57	76v		

	Decani				Cantoris			
	M	C-t	T	B	M	C-t	T	B
Patrick (Nathaniel) *1595								
Morning and Evening Service in G minor	37	34	38	32	39v	41	37v	35v
Communion Service in G minor	50	40v	44	38	45	51v	44v	41
Peerson (Martin) 1571/3 - 1651								
Blow out the trumpet	42	54	53	52v				
Portman (Richard) *c1655								
Service in G	26	23v	25	23	29v	28v	28	26
Lord, who shall dwell in thy tabernacle?	100v	92v	86	86	69v	85v		
Rejoice in the Lord, O ye righteous	108v	97v	91v	91v	74	88v	69	74
Purcell (Henry) 1659 - 1695								
Service in B flat	60v	48v	62	46v	61v	60	51v	52v
Behold, I bring you glad tidings		60v		57v	55v		86v	
Blessed be the Lord my strength	79v	105	98	101v	77v	79	73	77v
Blow up the trumpet	87v	103v	97	101	83v	97	78v	82v
Give sentence with me				55v				
I was glad	113		61	55v			81	
I will sing unto the Lord	69v	72	97v	68v		97v		
Let God arise	111	104		101v	59v	72v	59v	50
O give thanks (Ps,106)	82	59		56v			84v	
O God, the king of glory	62v	56v	56	55v				
O God, thou art my God					85v	74	86 88	69v
O God, thou hast cast us out					86v	98v	89	51v 71

	Decani				Cantoris			
	M	C-t	T	B	M	C-t	T	B
O Lord our governor	109v	100	93v	96	75v	90v		75v
O praise the Lord, all ye heathen	113	108	102	108v	56v	67v	78v	50v
Save me, O God (Ps.54)	70v	73	61v	68v				
Thy way, O God, is holy	79	58		70			56	
Thy word is a lantern		64v		72v	87			
Ramsey (Robert) fl c1612 – 1644								
Inclina, Domine	77	74v	65	74v	61	74v	56	67v
O come, let us sing unto the Lord	67v	69	59v	66	58v	72	58	49
Read (–?–) ? – ?								
Evening Service			28v					
Rogers (Benjamin) 1614 – 1698								
Evening Service in A minor	72v					66	52v	51
Short Service in D	16v	16v	18v	16	19v	19v	20	17v
Service in E minor	35v	32v	36	31	37 / 38v	39	35v	34
Service in G	31v	29	32	27v	32v	34v	31v	29v
Behold, I bring you glad tidings	96	86	70		67			
Behold now, praise the Lord	18	17v	19v	17	21	21	21	19
I beheld, and lo! a great multitude	71v					98	82	66v
O clap your hands	78v	57v / 58		69v			83v / 84	
O give thanks (Ps. 107)	96v		53v					
Teach me, O Lord	62	56	56	55				

	Decani				Cantoris			
	M	C-t	T	B	M	C-t	T	B
Sargenson (John) ? - ?								
Blessed is the man (Ps.1)	72		65v			73		70v
Smith (Edward) ? -*1612								
O praise God in his holiness		82v	81v			82v		
Strogers (Nicholas) fl 1560 - 1575								
Short Service	6v	6v	8v	5v	7v	7	8	5v
O God, be merciful unto us	38v	51	50	50				
Tallis (Thomas) c1505 - 1585								
Short Service	5	5	7 / 107	4	6	5	6	4
Blessed be thy name, O God	65	67	57	64		68		
I call and cry	65	67v	57v	64		68v		
O Lord, give thy holy spirit	38v	51	50	50				
With all our hearts	65	67	57	64		68		
Taylor (Silas) 1624 - 1678								
God is our hope and strength					82	96	77v	81
Tomkins (John) 1586 - 1638								
The king shall rejoice	70	76v	64	75v	60	75v		50v
Tomkins (Thomas) 1572 - 1656								
Short Service in C	10	10v	12v	9v	14	11v	12v	9v
Second Service in D minor	27v	24v	26v	24	31	30	29v	28
Almighty God, the fountain of all wisdom	68	70	60	66v		70		

	Decani				Cantoris			
	M	C-t	T	B	M	C-t	T	B
My beloved spake	93	84	79v	78	67v			
O Lord, I have loved the habitation	70	73		68v		67v	60	
O Lord, let me know mine end		81	75v			81v		
Thou art my king, O God	93	82	79			82		
Tucker (William) *1679								
Short Service in D minor	44	36	39v	34v	42v	43	39	39
'Benedicite' Service in F	42v			33v	41			37v 39
Comfort ye, my people	83v 100	101	72	95v		90		
I am well pleased	106	100v	93v	97v	66v		70v	76v
I was glad	106	96	90v	89v	72			
I will magnify thee	101	96	90	89				
Lord, how long wilt thou be angry?		99	85v	85v	65v	84v	71	76
My heart is fixed	69v	100v	94	96v	59v	72v	59v	50
O clap your hands	44v 69	72	61	68	58v			
O give thanks (Ps. 105)	103v	71	55v	55	71			
O give thanks (Ps. 107)	100v	94	87v	67v 87v				
Praise the Lord, ye servants	109	101v	85v	35v	75	85		
This is the day	95	98v	93	94v	69	89v		
Unto thee, O Lord, do I lift up		85	69v	83v	71v			
Wherewithal shall a young man cleanse?	104	94	88	88				
Tudway (Thomas) c1650 - 1726								
Behold, God is my salvation	79v	78	99	103	77		72	77v

	Decani				Cantoris			
	M	C-t	T	B	M	C-t	T	B
Blessed is the people								
My God, my God, look upon me	109	98	92v	94	55v	97v		
Turner (William) 1651 – 1740								
Behold, God is my salvation	86	87	96	82				
Behold, how good and joyful a thing	85	54v	53v					
By the waters of Babylon	86v	91	84					
Hear my prayer, O Lord (Ps. 102)	81	73, 74			84v	73	80v	83v
Lord, thou hast been our refuge	79v	105v	98v	102v				
Lord, what is man?	102v	93	86v	87	70v	87	67v	73
O be joyful in God	84	88v	88v			83		
O Lord God of hosts	62	72v	56v	104v	53v	59		
O praise the Lord (Ps. 147)	83, 86	91	71v					
O sing unto the Lord for it is a good thing							6?	
Sing, O daughter of Zion	42v, 85v, 83v	54	53v	53v				
Sing unto the Lord, O ye kingdoms		90	70				60v	84
The earth is the Lord's	83v	86, 89	83v			83	66v	
This is the day	84	89v	70				60v	
Try me, O God	113v	62	66	58	85v	66v	88	70v
Tye (Christopher) c1505 – ?1572								
I lift my heart to thee	66v	68	58v	65		69		
I will exalt thee (with 2nd part, Sing unto the Lord)	39v	51v	50v	50v				

	Decani				Cantoris			
	M	C-t	T	B	M	C-t	T	B
Ward (John) 1571 - c1638								
Bow down thine ear	94v	84v	76v					
I will magnify thee (See Cutts above)								
I will praise the Lord	88v	78	80	80v		91v		
Let God arise	98	81v	81	92v		81v		75
Weelkes (Thomas) *1623								
O Lord, grant the king a long life				76v				
White (Robert) c1538 - 1574 or (William) c1585 - 1625								
The Lord bless us (?Robert)	68v	71v	60v	68		71v		
O praise God in his holiness (?William)	74v	77	65v	73v	61v	76	55v	69
Wilkinson (Thomas or William) fl.1574 - 96								
Hear my prayer, O Lord, and let thine ear	97	83	82v	82v		81v		
O Jerusalem, thou that killest the prophets	67v	69v	59v	66	59	70v	58v	49
Preserve me, O Lord	97v 98v		82			72		
Why art thou so full of heaviness?	67v	69v	59v	66v	59	70v	58v	49
Wise (Michael) c1648 - 1687								
Morning and Evening Service in D minor	51v	41v	45v	39v	47	52v	46	42v
Communion Service in D minor	56v	57	102v	44	51v	57	49	46v
Communion Service in E	57	46	102v	44	51v			
Awake, put on thy strength	113	108	101v	108v				
Awake up my glory	104v	94v	88v	88				
Blessed is he that considereth the poor	107v	97	91	80	73			

	Decani				Cantoris			
	M	C-t	T	B	M	C-t	T	B
Blessed is the man (Ps. 1)	102v	93	86	86v	70v	87	67	72v
By the waters of Babylon	107	96v	90v	90	72v			
Have pity on me	71	73v			84		80	83v
How are the mighty fallen	105	95v	89	88v			82v	69
I will sing a new song	81v							
O praise God in his holiness	78	108v		69		67	82v	66v
Prepare ye the way	77v	108v		109			83v	
The Lord said unto my Lord	79	57v		69v			84	

Appendix I

The Westminster Abbey-Tucker-Bing connection.

As noted in the Introduction (p.6 supra), Bing was paid
for copying music for Westminster Abbey in the 1670's.
Furthermore, his own set of part-books now at York include
such annotations as 'as its in Mr Tucker's Books' and 'as
its in ye West (Westminster) Books'. William Tucker, Minor
Canon of Westminster Abbey and Gentleman of the Chapel Royal,
who died in February 1678/9, did a good deal of music copy-
ing both for the Abbey and for the Chapel Royal;[1] and if
Bing's further notes such as 'in ye Ch Books' and 'ye K
Books' do in fact refer to the 'Chapel' and to the 'King's'
Books, it may well have been through his Abbey colleague
Tucker that he obtained sight of these.

Survivals of Tucker's Chapel Royal work are available as
follows:

(a) The Chapel part-books now in the Music Room of the
British Library (Reference Division), RM 27.a.1-6.[2]

(b) A single Bass part-book, now Add.MS 50860 in the
British Library (Reference Division).

(c) A single Bass chorus part-book now in the Nanki Music
Library, Tokyo, Call No.N-5/10.

(d) Portions of an Organ book now in the Fitzwilliam
Museum. Cambridge (Music Ms 152).[3]

Of these (b) and (c), though differing in format (the one
upright folio, the other smaller oblong) may well be connect-
ed with the set of 'Anthems with Symphonies' mentioned in
footnote 1, page 94. A repertory of anthems of that character
having no relevance for Bing, the contents of these two MSS
are not of interest strictly for present purposes. (Nanki N-5/10
contains a few non-'Symphony' anthems added after the portion
copied by Tucker.) However, information about them not being
readily accessible, a summary account is given in Appendix
III infra. As to (a), the following Services and anthems are
still to be found in the Chapel Royal Books RM27.a.1-6 on

pages in Tucker's hand surviving from what must have been
many more written by him but now perished. Everything except
Purcell's 'Lord, who can tell?' is found in Bing's books.

Aldrich	Service in E minor
	Service in G
Amner	O come hither (ending)
Blow	Service in G
	O God, wherefore art thou absent?
	O how amiable are thy dwellings
	O Lord, thou hast searched me out
	Save me, O God (Ps. 69)
	The Lord hear thee
Child	Service in A minor
	Service in E minor (incomplete)
	O Lord, rebuke me not
Humfrey	Haste thee, O God
	Hear, O heavens
	Like as the hart
	Lord, teach us to number
Locke	Lord, let me know mine end
Purcell	Lord, who can tell how oft
Tucker	O give thanks (Ps. 107)
Turner	Lord, thou hast been our refuge
Wise	Awake, put on thy strength

A more copious repertory on Tucker's hand is still extant
in two part-books at Westminster Abbey, Alto Cantoris 'No 1A'
and Tenor Cantoris 'No 4', which correspond to each other
in their contents.[4] It will readily be observed how much
of this is to be found in Bing's set at York: only Aldrich's
'If the Lord himself' and Blow's 8-part 'God is our hope'
are not common to both.

Aldrich	Service in G
	If the Lord himself
Batten	Let my complaint
Blow	Service in E minor
	Service in G
	Behold, how good and joyful
	Christ rising again
	Lord, how are they increased
	God is our hope and strength (a 8)
	O how amiable are thy dwellings
	O God, wherefore art thou absent?
	O Lord, I have sinned
	O Lord, thou hast searched me out
	Save me, O God (Ps.69)
	Sing we merrily
	The Lord hear thee
	Turn thee unto me

Child	Service in A minor
	Service in E minor
	'Flat Service in E'
	Behold, how good and joyful
	O Lord, rebuke me not
	The earth is the Lord's
	Thou art my king, O God
Ferrabosco	Evening Service
C.Gibbons	The Lord said unto my Lord
Humfrey	Service in E minor
	By the waters of Babylon
	Haste thee, O God
	Hear, O heavens
	Like as the hart
	Lord, teach us to number our days
	O be joyful in the Lord
	O give thanks (Ps.118)
	O Lord my God
	Rejoice in the Lord, O ye righteous
W.Lawes	Let God arise
Locke	Not unto us
Purcell	Blessed be the Lord my strength
	Blow up the trumpet
	I will sing unto the Lord
	Let God arise
	O God, the king of glory
	O Lord our governor
Rogers	I beheld, and lo! a great multitude
	O clap your hands
Tucker	Benedicite Service
	Evening Service
	Comfort ye
	I am well pleased
	I was glad
	I will magnify thee
	Lord, how long wilt thou be angry?
	My heart is fixed
	O clap your hands
	O give thanks (Ps.105)
	This is the day
	Wherewithal shall a young man
Tudway	Behold, God is my salvation
Turner	Lord, thou hast been our refuge
Wise	Awake up, my glory
	How are the mighty fallen
	O praise God in his holiness
Humfrey	
Turner &	I will alway give thanks
Blow	

It should be said that though the musical notation of
these works is in Tucker's hand, he employed assistants to

help with the verbal text. What is a particularly interesting feature from the present point of view is that at the front of both books a separate single leaf has been inserted before what was originally the first item, Blow's Benedicite Service. Each of these single leaves carries 'Dr Blow's Te Deum to his Benedicite Service' and is in the hand not of Tucker but of Bing (in the style of Plate II), who must have added this between the date of Blow's doctorate (December 1677) and his own death. Again, following the last item transcribed by Tucker in each book (Thomas Tomkins's 'Let my complaint'), Bing takes up his pen and adds 'Dr Blow's Kyrie & Creed to his Service in Gamut' on the next pages.

All subsequent items is these books are post-Tucker/Bing, but Bing himself makes an interesting appearance in a third Westminster part-book, Tenor Decani '5'. This is now a composite volume into which, for economy's sake four groups of older leaves from some earlier were built. These four groups, which are not contiguous to each other, contain the following items by Bing (also in the style of Plate II) in the order here shown:

A. Thomas Tomkins   *Second Service (beginning in the middle of 8)
   Portman   *Service in G (2,4,6,7,8,10)
   Bryne   *Service in G (2,5,6,7,8,10)
   Rogers   *Behold, now praise the Lord
   Child   *Service in D (2,5,6,7,8,10)
                          *Service in F (2,5,6,7,9,11)
                          *'Benedicite' Service in G (3,5,6,7,8,10,2)

B. Patrick   *Service in G minor (part of 2,4,6,7,part of 8)
   Blow   *Service in A (part of 2,5,6,7,9,11)
   Orlando Gibbons   +Second Service (8,10)

C. Tye   *+(Ending of) I will exalt thee (with 2nd
                             part, Sing unto the Lord)
   William Mundy   *+O Lord, the maker of all thing
   William Mundy   *+O Lord, the world's saviour
   Hooper   *+Teach me thy way
   Orlando Gibbons   *+Almighty and everlasting God
   Batten   *+O praise the Lord, all ye heathen
                           *+Haste thee, O God (with 2nd part)
                           *+When the Lord turned again the captivity
                           *Deliver us, O Lord our God
                           *My soul truly waiteth

(vertical annotation alongside group C: This sequence in the York books)

Child		*Praise the Lord, O my soul (Ps.103)
		*O Lord, grant the king a long life
		*If the Lord himself
Batten		Sing joyfully
Child		*O pray for the peace of Jerusalem
Rogers		*Teach me, O Lord

D. Tallis ⎡*+With all our hearts
Hooper │*+Blessed be thy name, O God
William Mundy │*+O thou God, Almighty Father
Tallis │*+O Lord, I bow the knees
Byrd │*+I call and cry
Hooper │*+Prevent us, O Lord
⎣*+Behold, it is Christ

(left bracket label) This sequence in the York books

(right bracket label) This sequence in Barnard

*In Bing's hand in the books now at York

+In Barnard's First Book of Selected Church Musick (1641)

References to Appendix I

1. WAM 33712. 1677: 'To Mr Tucker for Coppying out some Musick bookes for the use of the Church xl'; 'To him more on the like Occassion xl.' £20 must have represented a considerable amount of work, going back probably more than one year. At the time of his death a sum of £15 was owing to him for 'writing in 15 books the Anthems with Symphonies for King Charles the 2nds use in his Chappell Royal'. See J.Y.Akerman, Moneys. . .for Secret Service of Charles II and James II (Camden Society, London, 1851), p.98.

2. These, formerly RM 23.m.1-6, were discussed by me in 'A Contemporary Source of English Music of the Purcellian Period', Acta Musicologica, vol.31 (1959), pp.38-44. I subsequently identified Tucker as the scribe of the items which I there listed from 'the first group of older leaves'. A further nine books have come to light recently so that the whole set is now collectively known as RM 27.a.1-15, but only the first six books preserve a record of Tucker's activity.

3. See my paper, 'A Cambridge Manuscript from the English Chapel Royal', Music & Letters, vol.42 (1961), pp.263-7.

4. It is very possible that these books were among those at Westminster Abbey known to Vincent Novello long ago but thereafter overlooked until Dr Douglas Guest found them among choir music and passed them to the Abbey Library. See The Cathedral Service, Anthems. . . by Henry Purcell, edited by Vincent Novello, 4 vols, London, 1828.

Appendix II

The St Paul's Cathedral-Bing-Gostling connection

Six part-books survive at St Paul's Cathedral containing
material copied c1675-c1700. Two of them (Contratenor and
Tenor Decani) are devoted to Services, the others (Contratenor, Tenor, and Bass Decani; Bass Cantoris) to Anthems.

The two books of Services are very largely in the hand
of Bing of the character of Plate II, but one or two pages
are missing, and one or two others, inserted no doubt to
make good some damaged passages, are in a much later hand.
The repertory of the Bing sections of both books, which
may be compared with that of the York books, is as follows:

Aldrich	E minor (Benedicite Service)
	G
Batten	Short
Bevin	Short
Bryne	Short
Blow	A
	E minor (Benedicite Service)
Byrd	Short
Child	A minor
	E minor
	'Flat Service in E'
	F
	G (Benedicite Service)
	Verse Evening Service in G
Farrant (J.)	Short
Farrant (R.)	'High'
Gibbons (O.)	Short
Humfrey	E minor
Patrick	G minor
Portman	G
Rogers	E minor (Verse)
	D
	G
Tomkins (T.)	C
	D minor (Second Service)
Tucker	F (Benedicite Service)

It appears that at the point when he reached the two
Services of Aldrich and that by Tucker, Bing had come to
the end of his time. In the Tenor Decani book all three
are in his writing, Aldrich being designated 'Mr', as

indeed he was up to Bing's death. But some slight change of
hand can be discerned in these works in the Contratenor book,
and this appears on inspection to be that of John Gostling
endeavouring to match Bing's style as much as possible, in
particular in the downward stems of the notes and the avoid-
ance of the typically Gostling backward-looped 'd'. Moreover,
in this book Aldrich appears as 'Dr', a status he acquired
on 2 March 1681/2, that is to say after Bing's death. In due
course the characteristically personal hand of Gostling
asserts itself. His contribution to these books is therefore:

Aldrich	in E minor (Contratenor only)
	G (Contratenor only)
Blow	E minor (Contratenor only)
Purcell	B flat
Rogers	A minor
Wise	D minor (Contratenor only)

The four anthem books as they now stand are 'cannibalised';
that is to say when they were constituted in the 18th century
substantial sections from earlier books were built into them.
Those earlier sections, which may be differentiated from the
later at a mere glance, are in John Gostling's hand, long
stretches being in that style, as noticed in the Service
books, accommodating itself to Bing's but giving place event-
ually to his personal manner. The repertory of those sections
is rather too extensive, even if relevant, to be set out here,
but in summary it is closely on the lines of Bing's anthology
(from which much of the text may indeed have been derived),
with a few later works by Blow and Purcell added.

It stops short of anything of the Clarke and Croft gener-
ation. Quite early in the Full Anthem part of the Contratenor
Decani book there is Byrd's 'O Lord, make thy servant William,
our king', which could not have been entered at the earliest
before 1688 and more probably not until 1694 or after; and
no more than some ten items further on we reach Blow's 'My
God, my God, look upon me' which was not composed until

6 September, 1697. One therefore judges that this extensive
amount of copying by Gostling represents concentrated work
in the period 1695-1700 when the reconstituted choir of
the Cathedral once more became fully active, more particularly after the opening of the Choir of Wren's building
in 1697.

Appendix III

Chapel Royal Part-books of 'Anthems with Symphonies'
in the hand of William Tucker (February 1678/9)

(A)   British Museum (Reference Division), Add. MS 50860.
Bass part. Upright folio with royal arms on front cover
and what appears to be the youthful signature of W.Crofts
(sic) with date 1697 inside back cover. Formerly belonging
to Richard Border and W.H.Cummings. In three items Tucker
has employed an assistant to help with the verbal text.
Some pages of the book are now missing.

(B)   Nanki Library, Tokyo, N-5/10. Bass chorus part. Small
oblong. Formerly belonging to W.H.Cummings and E.J.Hopkins.
The book has been scrawled upon by (apparently) Chapel
Royal choristers, among them Edmund Baker, later organist
of Chester Cathedral, whose voice had changed by 28 December 1710. In several places Tucker has employed an assistant to help with the verbal text, one of them being the
same as in (A) above. This book has extensive additions
made after Tucker's work, and some pages are now missing.
In the list below, only items with which Tucker had to do
are mentioned.

An intriguing feature of (B) is the endorsement on the
page devoted to the 'Club' Anthem:
      Compos'd by Pell; Humfrey. Will: Turner. John Blow
The two last names are certainly in the form of autograph
signatures of the two composers, and the words 'Compos'd

by Pell: Humfrey' may possibly be in Humfrey's writing. If
so, the endorsement must date from between about mid-April
1674 and his death (having made his Will on 23 April) on 14
July of that year, because only five pages earlier occurs
Blow's 'When Israel came out of Egypt', which was composed
on 5 April 1674 (Bodleian Library, MS Mus. Sch. c.39, p.112
and c.58, f.9v).

Blow	And I heard a great voice	A	B
	Arise, O Lord		B
	I beheld, and lo! a great multitude	A	B
	Sing we merrily		B
	the kings of Tharsis		B
	The Lord is my shepherd	A	B
	When Israel came out of Egypt	A	B
	When the Lord turned again	A	
Humfrey	By the waters of Babylon	A	B
	Haste thee, O God	A	B
	Hear my crying	A	B
	O be joyful	A	
	O give thanks (Ps.118)	A	B
	O praise the Lord, laud ye	A	
	Rejoice in the Lord, O ye righteous	A	B
	The king shall rejoice		B
	Thou art my king, O God	A	B
Humfrey Turner Blow	I will alway give thanks		B
Locke	God is gone up	A	B
	God reigneth		B
	O clap your hands together	A	B
Purcell	If the Lord himself	A	B
	My beloved spake	A	
	Praise the Lord, ye servants	A	B
Tudway	O come let us sing unto the Lord	A	
Turner	Hold not thy tongue, O God		B
	O praise the Lord (Psalm 147)	A	B